BMC (Leyland)
1.5 + 1.8 Litre Diesel Engines
Operation and Repair Manuals

BMC (Leyland)

1.5 + 1.8 Litre Diesel Engines

Operation and Repair Manuals

EAB/ISBN: 978-3-86195-260-2

Published in 2010 by Europaeischer Hochschulverlag GmbH & Co. KG, Fahrenheitstr. 1, D-28359 Bremen (www.tecbooks.net). All rights reserved to the Publisher and its Licensors.

BMC (Leyland)
1.5 + 1.8 Litre Diesel Engines
Operation and Repair Manuals

CONTENT

BMC (LEYLAND) 1,5 + 1.8 LITRE DIESEL ENGINE OPERATORS MANUAL   1

BMC (LEYLAND) 1.5 LITRE DIESEL REPAIR OPERATION MANUAL   28

BMC (LEYLAND) 1.8 LITRE DIESEL REPAIR OPERATION MANUAL   60

BMC (LEYLAND)

1,5 LITRE DIESEL ENGINE

1,8 LITRE DIESEL ENGINE

OPERATION MANUAL

CONTENTS

RUNNING INSTRUCTIONS

COOLING SYSTEM

ELECTRICAL

FUEL SYSTEM

ENGINE

    MARINE ENGINES
        Laying up
        Recommissioning

    INDUSTRIAL ENGINES
        Storage
        Recommissioning

FAULT DIAGNOSIS

GENERAL DATA

MAINTENANCE SUMMARY

LUBRICATION

SERVICE

RUNNING INSTRUCTIONS

Starting the engine Check that the gear lever is in the neutral position, fully open the throttle and operate the starter switch. Release the starter switch and close the throttle as soon as the engine is running. For cold starting proceed as for normal starting, but before operating the starter switch, switch on the heater plugs for a period of between 15 and 30 seconds. Release the heater plug switch as soon as the engine starts. The heater plug elements will be rapidly destroyed if they are kept switched on while the engine is running.

NOTE: The use of ether starting aids is not recommended.

Starter Do not operate the starter for more than one minute at a time. If the engine has failed to start after 30 seconds' pre-heat and one minute cranking, wait three minutes before again attempting to start the engine.

Stopping the engine Operate the stop control to cut off the supply of fuel to the injection pump, then the engine will cease firing.

Running-in The following instructions should be strictly adhered to during the first 25 hours' running:

Do not exceed 2,500 rev/min.

Do not operate at full load at any speed.

Between 25 and 50 hours gradually increase the load and speed up to the full rating for the engine.

After 50 hours' running change the engine oil and oil filter, see page 12 and 1·8 diesel only: Retorque the cylinder head nuts to 102 Nm (72 lbf ft, 10·4 kgf m) in the sequence shown (see Fig. 1), using service tool 18G 694 A.

Check the valve rocker clearances, see page 13.

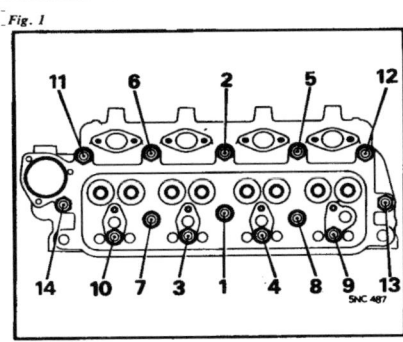

Fig. 1

NOTE: In the case of pump, generator and other constant speed applications, if the engine has not been run-in by the equipment manufacturer, gradually increase the load on the engine during the first 25 to 40 hours; or run the engine for short periods, starting at 15 minutes, gradually increasing up to constant running at 30 to 40 hours.

Warming up Run the engine at a fast idling speed (approx. 1,500 rev/min) until the engine attains its normal working temperature. Do not allow the engine to idle slowly.

Avoid prolonged idling or high no-load engine speeds.

Check the engine oil pressure and coolant temperature frequently.

COOLING SYSTEM

Frost precautions   Water expands when it freezes, and if precautions are not taken there is considerable risk of bursting the radiator or cylinder block; it is therefore essential to use anti-freeze in the cooling system in freezing conditions.

We recommend the use of **UNIPART** universal anti-freeze to protect the cooling system.

If **UNIPART** universal is not available any anti-freeze conforming to specification B.S. 3151 or B.S. 3152 may be used. Anti-freezes to these specifications are compatible with **UNIPART** universal and can be used with it. **UNIPART** universal should not be mixed with other universal anti-freezes.

After filling with anti-freeze solution, attach a warning label to a prominent position stating the type of anti-freeze contained in the cooling system to ensure that the correct type is used for topping-up.

Anti-freeze can remain in the cooling system for two years provided that the specific gravity of the coolant is checked periodically and anti-freeze added as necessary. After the second year the system should be drained and flushed by inserting a hose in the filling orifice and allowing water to flow through until clean. Make sure that the cooling system is water-tight, examine all joints and replace any defective hose with a new one. Refill with the appropriate anti-freeze solution.

The recommended solutions of anti-freeze, are given below.

Solution	Commences to freeze		Frozen solid	
%	°C	°F	°C	°F
25	−13	9	−26	−15
33¼	−19	−2	−36	−33
50	−36	−33	−48	−53

Draining   To drain the cooling system, remove the plug or open the tap located in the right-hand side of the cylinder block and disconnect the lowest hose in the cooling system.

ELECTRICAL

Alternator **NOTE: The alternator needs no maintenance attention apart from external cleaning and must not be lubricated.**

Polarity. Ensure that the correct battery polarity is maintained at all times. Reversed battery or charger connections will damage the alternator rectifiers.

Battery connections. The battery must never be disconnected while the engine is running.

Testing semi-conductor devices. Never use an ohmmeter of the type incorporating a hand-driven generator for checking the rectifiers or the transistors.

Welding. If arc welding is to be carried out on the vehicle, the alternator and battery must be disconnected. When welding, brazing or soldering ensure that any heat is kept away from the alternator.

FUEL SYSTEM

Fuel oils Fuel oils suitable for use in this diesel engine are generally known as Diesel fuel oil, distillate Diesel fuel, automative gas oil or Derv fuel. Users are recommended to obtain their supplies from a source which can be depended upon to maintain a consistent standard of quality. Waste or residual oils of any sort are to be avoided. It is recommended that the fuel should conform to British Standard 2869: 1967, Class A1 or A2.

Air cleaner element Unscrew the wing nut, remove the cover and discard the element. Thoroughly clean the container, fit a new element, replace the cover, ensure the sealing ring is in good condition and replace the air cleaner, fit the fibre washer and tighten the nut.

NOTE: These instructions apply to vehicle type paper elements. For other air cleaner types refer to the equipment manufacturer.

Roadside adjustment
Fig. 1 Do not undertake any dismantling of the injectors or injection pump at the roadside. Renewing an injector (1) is the only servicing of this nature which can be carried out at the roadside (see 'Fuel injectors', page 10). To locate a faulty injector, slacken the feed pipe union nut (2) on the suspect injector and run the engine slowly. If there is no change in the engine performance or if a faulty condition, such as a smoky exhaust, has disappeared, it can be assumed that the injector is faulty.

Heater plugs
Fig. 2 Remove the electrical leads (1) and unscrew each plug (2) from the cylinder head. Insert a twist drill (3) of 4·37 mm (11/64 in) diameter into the screwed holes (4) in the head and turn the drill by hand to remove the carbon build-up. Withdraw the drill and remove any particles of carbon from the conical seatings in the cylinder head. Refit the heater plugs and electrical leads.

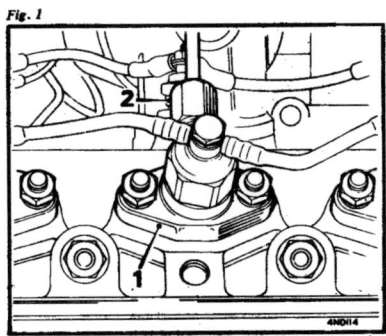

Fig. 1

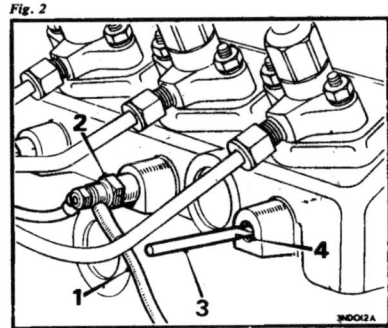

Fig. 2

Bleeding the fuel system
Fig. 3

Air can enter the fuel system if any part of the system is dismantled or through an air leak in the system. This can result in failure to start or erratic engine acceleration.

To rectify, bleed the system as follows:

(a) Slacken the blanking plug (1) and the screw union (2) on the filter head.
(b) Slacken the union nut (3) and the air bleed screws (4, 5 and 6).
(c) Slacken the union nuts at the injector end of the high-pressure pipes.
(d) Operate the lift pump manual priming lever until the fuel flowing from the blanking plug (1) is free from air bubbles; tighten the plug.
(e) Continue operating the priming lever until the fuel flowing from screws (2, 3, 4 and 5) are free from air bubbles; tighten each screw in turn.
(f) Crank the engine until the fuel flowing from the screw (6) is free from air bubbles; tighten the screw.
(g) Continue cranking the engine until the fuel from at least two injectors is free from air bubbles; tighten the injector unions.
(h) Start the engine, and allow it to run until it is firing on all cylinders.

NOTE: Bleed point (6) is not fitted to some engine specifications.

After renewing the fuel filter element, it will only be necessary to bleed the fuel filter points (1 and 2) provided that the engine has not been cranked while the filter is dismantled.

WARNING: Do not attempt to bleed the system by towing a vehicle in gear as this would result in serious damage to the injection pump.

Accelerator Lubricate the accelerator control linkage.

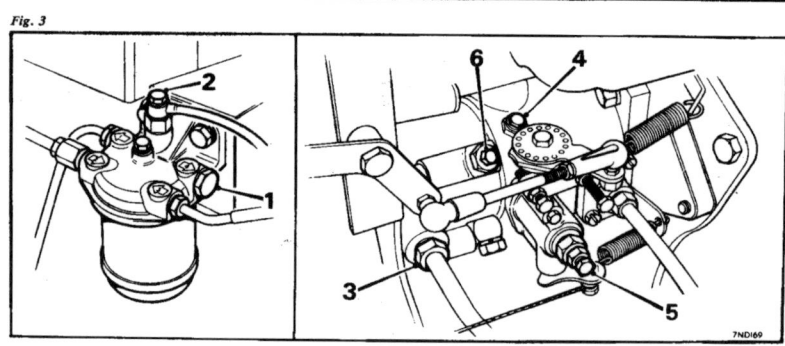
Fig. 3

Fuel System

Fuel injectors
Fig. 4
Injector cleaning and spray testing can only be carried out with specialized equipment. To remove an injector, disconnect the high pressure pipe (1) from the individual injector (2), and the leak-off pipe unions (3) from all the injectors. Note the seal washer either side of each banjo. Remove the two injector retaining nuts (4) and withdraw the injector. Extract the corrugated sealing washer (5) from inside the nozzle heat shield (6). Before refitting an injector fit a new sealing washer (5) as illustrated, and inspect the injector joint gasket (7) for serviceability. Tighten the two injector retaining nuts evenly and to the correct torque tightness (see 'GENERAL DATA'). Refit the high pressure feed pipe and leak-off pipes.

Main fuel filter
Fig. 5
To remove the filter element (1) unscrew the centre bolt (2) and support the filter base (3). Detach the base and twist the element to remove it from the filter head (4). Remove the three sealing washers (5) from the head and base. Clean the filter base, and reassemble the filter unit using a new filter element and sealing washers. The fuel system must be bled of air after dismantling and reassembling the filter unit.

Governor speeds
These should only be adjusted by a qualified person and should be resealed after setting.

NOTE: Unauthorized adjustment of the fuel injection pump settings may invalidate the factory warranty.

Fuel injection equipment
NOTE: Further information and overhaul instructions for fuel injection equipment can be obtained from the maker's local agents (C.A.V./Simms), or from:
C.A.V. & Simms Service
C.A.V. Limited
P.O. Box 36
Warple Way
LONDON W3 7SS

Quote on application:
(a) Engine type and serial number.
(b) Fuel pump type and serial number.

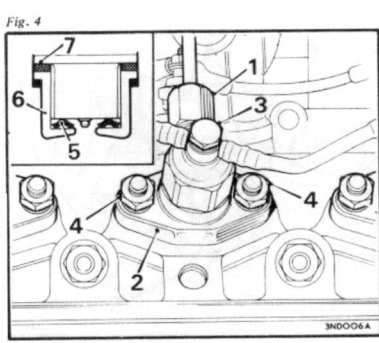
Fig. 4

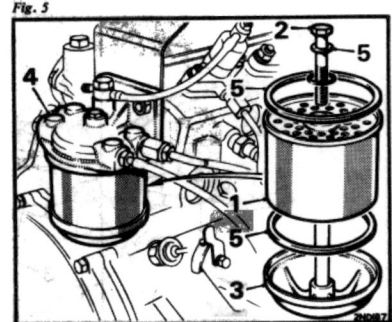
Fig. 5

ENGINE

Lifting When removing or refitting the engine always use an engine lifting bar (1) through
Fig. 1 the lifting eye brackets or by two long chains and a spreader bar.

Lubrication Check the sump oil level by removing the dipstick (1). Maintain the level between
Fig. 2, Fig. 3 the 'MAX' and 'MIN' marks and never allow it to fall below the 'MIN' mark. To
and Fig. 4 drain the sump oil remove the plug (2). Clean the plug before replacing it. Turn
the oil filler cap (3) anti-clockwise to remove. Fill the sump with new oil until the
dipstick registers the correct level. The sump is best drained when the engine is
warm.

The oil filler cap incorporates a filter for the closed-circuit crankcase breathing
intake. The cap and filter are renewed only as a complete assembly.

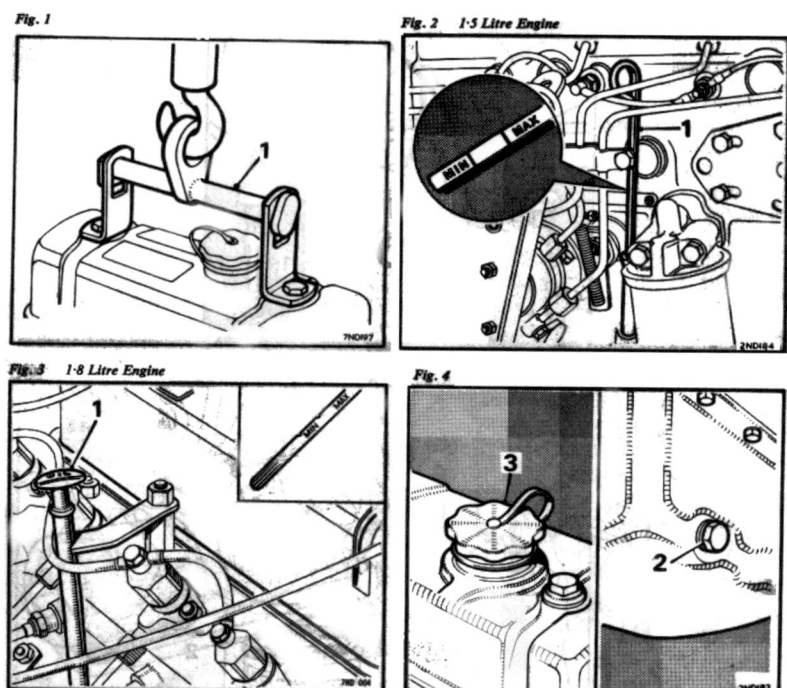

Fig. 1

Fig. 2 1·5 Litre Engine

Fig. 3 1·8 Litre Engine

Fig. 4

Engine

Injection pump driving gears
Fig. 5

1·5 Litre Engine: Withdraw the driving gear lubricator (1) and filter gauze (2) and clean in petrol (gasoline). Use a stiff brush to clean the gauze, and blow out the lubricator with compressed air. Refit, ensuring that the copper joint washers (3) are serviceable. Check for oil leaks after running the engine.

Oil filter
Fig. 6

1·5 Litre Engine: Remove the central bolt (1) and lower the bowl (2). Remove and discard the filter element (3). Clean out the bowl with petrol (gasoline), allow to dry, fit a new element, and reassemble the bowl to the filter head (4). Note the order of assembly of the components, as illustrated. Ensure that the bowl sealing gasket (5) is serviceable.

Fig. 7

1·8 Litre Engine: Unscrew the old filter cartridge (1) from the filter head (3) and discard it. Smear the seal (2) of the new filter cartridge with oil and locate on the filter head. Screw on and tighten the cartridge with the hands only.

DO NOT USE A SPANNER TO TIGHTEN: DO NOT OVERTIGHTEN.

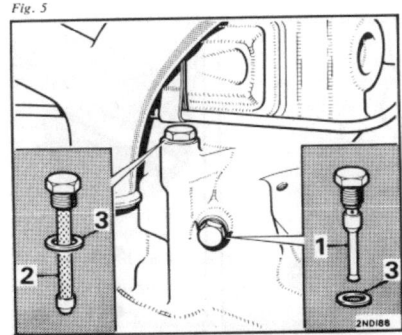

Fig. 5

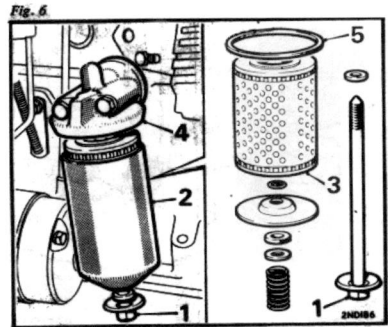

Fig. 6

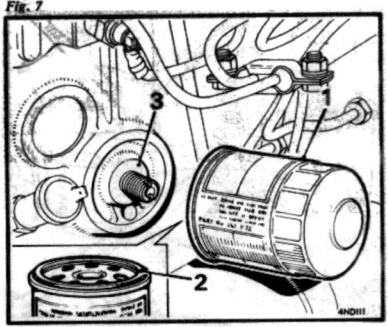

Fig. 7

Valve rockers The correct clearance between the valve rockers and the valve stem is given in
Fig. 8 **'GENERAL DATA'.** Unscrew the rocker cover retaining nuts (1) and lift off the cover.

Check the clearance at the position illustrated and in the order as follows

Check No. 1 valve with No. 8 fully open. Check No. 8 valve with No. 1 fully open.
,, ,, 3 ,, ,, ,, 6 ,, ,, ,, ,, 6 ,, ,, ,, 3 ,, ,,
,, ,, 5 ,, ,, ,, 4 ,, ,, ,, ,, 4 ,, ,, ,, 5 ,, ,,
,, ,, 2 ,, ,, ,, 7 ,, ,, ,, ,, 7 ,, ,, ,, 2 ,, ,,

Adjust, if necessary, by slackening the locking nut (2) and turning the adjusting screw (3) until the clearance is correct. Hold the screw against rotation and tighten the locking nut. Refit the rocker cover, checking that its cork gasket (4) is serviceable.

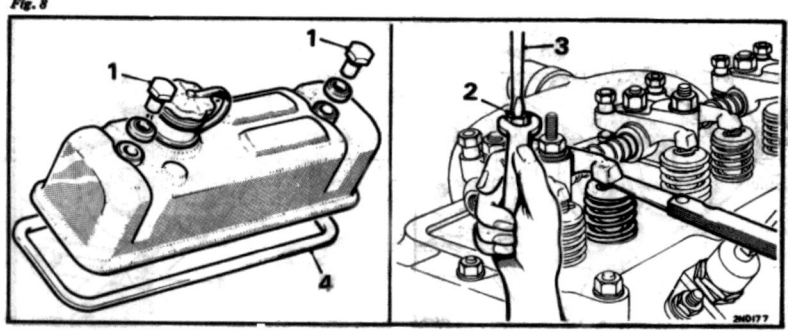

Fig. 8

Engine

Alternator Use one of the following methods of checking the belt tension:
Fig. 9 and
Fig. 10 (a) Use a torque spanner to apply a load of 14·9 to 15·6 Nm (11 to 11·5 lbf ft, 1·5 to 1·6 kgf m) in a clockwise direction to the alternator pulley retaining nut. If the belt tension is correct the belt will slip at this torque loading.

(b) Apply a load of 33·4 to 36·4 N (7·5 to 8·2 lbf, 3·3 to 3·6 kgf) at right angles to the belt midway between the pulleys. The belt should deflect 6 mm (0·25 in).

NOTE: Fit a new belt with a moderate degree of tension, run the engine for five minutes at 1,000 rev/min, stop the engine, then set the belt to the correct tension.

Do not apply leverage to any part of the alternator other than the drive end bracket.

Clean the slip-ring end cover ventilating apertures indicated by the arrow.

To adjust the belt tension, slacken the three alternator mounting bolts (1) and the nut (2) securing the adjusting link to the engine. Pull the alternator (3) outwards until the belt is correctly tensioned, then tighten the adjusting link nut and the three mounting bolts.

'Laying up' a If a marine engine is not to be used at least once a month during the winter, it is
marine engine strongly advised that the following procedure be adopted, or the current practice of the country concerned:

(a) Run the engine until normal operating temperature is reached, then stop the engine and change the engine oil and oil filter.

(b) Run the engine for two minutes at 1,500 rev/min with no load and stop the engine.

(c) Remove the injectors and pour 60 cc (⅛ pint) of engine oil into each cylinder. Rock the crankshaft backwards and forwards about a quarter turn each way to distribute the oil.

(d) Check the injectors, and renew if necessary, using new crimp washers under the injectors.

(e) Drain the cooling system (see page 6), leaving the hose disconnected.

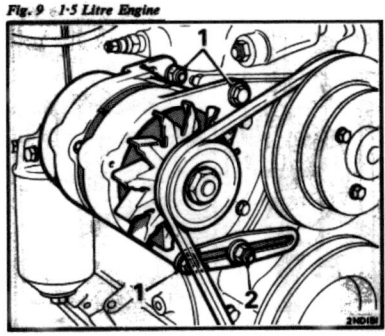

Fig. 9 1·5 Litre Engine

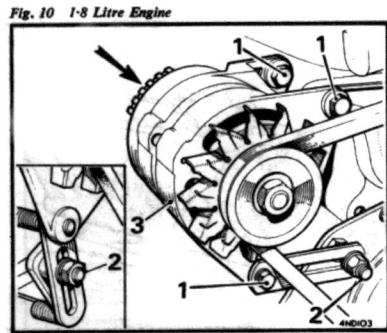

Fig. 10 1·8 Litre Engine

(f) Drain the raw water system including the impeller housing of the raw water pump.
(g) Seal all external outlets, the exhaust, air inlet, crankcase breather, etc.
(h) Turn off the fuel at the tank and the fuel return.
(i) Lubricate all the engine/gearbox controls, and lightly spray the power unit with oil or preservative.
(j) Remove the battery to a dry storage area and re-charge monthly.
(k) Apply waterproof grease to all electrical connections, and cover the alternator ventilation slots.
(l) It is advisable to fill the fuel tank before storage.

NOTE: If an engine is not 'laid up' and freezing conditions are possible, then a suitable anti-freeze mixture must be used in the cooling system (see page 6).

Recommissioning a 'laid-up' engine

It is important that this procedure is followed, otherwise severe damage to the engine may result.

(a) Clean the outside of the power unit with a suitable degreaser.
(b) Lubricate all linkages and controls.
(c) Remove all seals, covers and protective parts.
(d) Fit the batteries, which should have been freshly charged, ensuring they are connected correctly.
(e) Fill the cooling system after closing taps and re-connecting any hoses.
(f) Check drive belt tensions and conditions, renew or adjust as necessary.
(g) Check the engine oil level.
(h) Drain the fuel tank sediment trap completely.
(i) Open the fuel feed tap and return tap and drain the fuel line sedimenter.
(j) Rotate the engine slowly by hand and ensure the oil put in the cylinders before storage has drained down. If any strong resistance is present, remove the injectors, rotate by hand and check for the presence of excessive oil in the cylinders.

If any oil is present, turn over by hand at least 10 times, then crank using the starter motor to remove excess oil via the injector holes.

NOTE: the oil will be removed with considerable pressure and precautions should be taken to contain the oil discharged.

It is advisable to remove the injector heat shields before cranking.

Replace the injectors, ensuring new crimp washers and the injector heat shields are in place, see page 10.

(k) Crank the engine for a few seconds with the stop control in the off position and no pre-heat, apply a full 30 to 40 seconds pre-heat and start the engine in the normal manner.
(l) Check for oil pressure and raw water flow. Run the engine for 10 minutes at 1,500 rev/min at a light load.
(m) Stop the engine, check the oil levels, drive belt tensions, engine coolant level, fuel line, sedimenter, etc.

Engine

Storing an Industrial Engine

Where an engine is not to be used for at least two hours per month it should be stored as detailed below, or according to the current practice of the country concerned.

Engines on standby duty should be run for at least two hours per month under normal operating conditions. Where freezing conditions may be encountered always use anti-freeze mixture in the cooling system (see page 6).

(a) Run the engine until normal operating temperature is reached, then stop the engine and change the engine oil and oil filter.

(b) Run the engine at 1,500 rev/min or normal operating speed, then stop the engine.

(c) Remove the injectors and pour 60 cc ($\frac{1}{8}$ pint) of engine oil into each cylinder. Rock the crankshaft backwards and forwards about a quarter turn each way to distribute the oil.

(d) Check the injectors, and renew if necessary, using new crimp washers under the injectors.

(e) Drain the cooling system (see page 6), leaving the hose disconnected.

(f) Drain the external water system including the impeller housing of the external water pump, if fitted.

(g) Seal all external outlets, the exhaust, air inlet, crankcase breather, etc.

(h) Turn off the fuel at the tank and the fuel return.

(i) Lubricate all the engine controls and lightly spray the power unit with oil or preservative.

(j) Remove the battery to a dry storage area and re-charge monthly.

(k) Apply a waterproof grease to all electrical connections, and cover the alternator ventilation slots.

(l) It is also advisable to fill the fuel tank before storage.

Recommissioning a stored engine

It is important that this procedure is followed, otherwise severe damage to the engine may result.

(a) Clean the outside of the power unit with a suitable degreaser.

(b) Lubricate all linkages and controls.

(c) Remove all seals, covers and protective parts.

(d) Fit the batteries, which should have been freshly charged, ensuring they are connected correctly.

(e) Fill the cooling system after closing taps and re-connecting any hoses.

(f) Check drive belt tensions and conditions, renew or adjust as necessary.

(g) Check the engine oil level.

(h) Drain the fuel tank sediment trap completely.

(i) Open the fuel feed tap and return tap and drain the fuel line sediment.

(j) Rotate the engine slowly by hand and ensure the oil put in the cylinders before storage has drained down. If any strong resistance is present, remove the injectors, rotate by hand and check for the presence of excessive oil in the cylinders.

If any oil is present, turn over by hand at least 10 times, then crank using the starter motor to remove excess oil via the injector holes.

NOTE: the oil will be expelled with considerable pressure and precautions should be taken to contain the oil discharged.

It is advisable to remove the injector heat shields before cranking.

Replace the injectors, ensuring new crimp washers and the injector heat shields are in place, see page 10.

(k) Crank the engine for a few seconds with the stop control in the off position and no pre-heat, apply a full 30 to 40 seconds pre-heat and start the engine in the normal manner.

(l) Check for oil pressure and coolant flow. Run the engine for 10 minutes at 1,500 rev/min at a light load or normal operating speed.

(m) Stop the engine, check the oil levels, drive belt tensions, engine coolant level, fuel line, sedimenter, etc.

FAULT DIAGNOSIS

Listed below are various symptoms of irregular engine performance with their possible causes. Should the engine develop any of these faults which cannot be rectified after investigating the possible cause, consult your engine supplier.

Difficult starting
Start with check No. 1 and proceed as directed.

Misfiring
Start with check No. 25 and proceed as directed.

Incorrect idling
Start with check No. 22 and proceed as directed.

Excessive exhaust
Start with check No. 13 and proceed as directed.

Loss of power (Ensure that the vehicle/equipment is not overloaded). Start with check No. 30 and proceed as directed.

Check	Action
1. Is the cranking speed low?	Yes: Check 2. No: Check 6.
2. Is the engine oil of the correct grade?	Yes: Check 3. No: Change the engine oil.
3. Is the battery fully charged and in good condition?	Yes: Check 4. No: Change or re-charge the battery as necessary.
4. Are the connections in the starter circuit satisfactory?	Yes: Remove the starter and check 5. No: Make all starter circuit connections satisfactory.
5. Is the starter motor performance satisfactory on a test bench?	Yes: Investigate the engine for tightness. No: Overhaul or renew the starter motor.
6. Is the fuel reaching the injectors?	Yes: Check 13. No: Check 7.
7. Is the stop control correctly set and is its linkage free?	Yes: Check 8. No: Reset the control position or linkage as necessary.
8. Is there a supply of clean fuel in the tank?	Yes: Check 9. No: Refuel the tank and bleed the fuel system.
9. Are there leaks at fuel pipes or connections?	No: Check 10. Yes: Cure the leaks and bleed the fuel system.
10. Is there a blockage in the fuel system?	No: Check 11. Yes: Clear the blockage or renew the filter element as necessary, then bleed the fuel system.
11. Is the pump delivering fuel?	Yes: Check 12. No: Overhaul or renew the lift pump and bleed the fuel system.

Check	Action
12. Does the fuel system require bleeding?	No: Overhaul the injection pump. Yes: Bleed all air from the fuel system.
13. Are the injector pipes connected in their correct firing order?	Yes: Check 14. No: Correct the firing order and bleed the fuel system.
14. Are the correct injectors correctly fitted?	Yes: Check 15. No: Correct the error and bleed the fuel system.
15. Are the injection pump timing marks correctly aligned?	Yes: Check 16. No: Re-set the injection pump timing.
16. Is the air cleaner or induction system blocked?	No: Check 17. Yes: Clear the blockage or clean and re-oil the air filter.
17. Is the exhaust system restricted?	No: Remove the injectors and check 18. Yes: Clear the restriction.
18. Is the injector opening pressure and performance satisfactory?	Yes: Remove the injection pump and check 19. No: Overhaul or renew the injectors.
19. Is the injection timing pointer correctly positioned when checked with tool MS 67 A?	Yes: Check 20. No: Re-set the injection timing pointer.
20. Is the injection pump performance satisfactory on a test bench?	Yes: Check 21. No: Overhaul, or renew the injection pump.
21. Is the valve/rocker clearance and valve timing correct?	Yes: Investigate the engine for wear or damage causing lack of compression. Conduct a compression test. No: Correct the valve/rocker clearance and/or valve timing.
22. Does the throttle linkage interfere with the idling speed setting?	No: Check 23. Yes: Correct the throttle linkage adjustment.
23. Does the stop control linkage interfere with the position of the stop lever?	No: Check 24. Yes: Set the stop control linkage correctly.
24. Is the idling stop screw setting correct?	Yes: Check 25. No: Adjust the engine idling speed.
25. Is the fuel tank air vent restricted?	No: Check 26. Yes: Clear the fuel tank air vent.
26. Are there leaks at the fuel pipes or connections?	No: Check 27. Yes: Cure the leaks and bleed the fuel system.

Fault Diagnosis

Check	Action
27. Is there a blockage in the fuel system?	No: Check 28. Yes: Clear the blockage or renew the filter element as necessary then bleed the fuel system.
28. Does the fuel system require bleeding?	No: Check 29. Yes: Bleed all the air from the fuel system.
29. Is the lift pump delivery pressure above 36·2 kN/m^2 (0·37 kgf/cm^2, 5·25 lbf/in^2)?	Yes: Check 13. No: Overhaul or renew the lift pump.
30. Are the vehicle brakes binding?	No: Check 31. Yes: Adjust the brakes.
31. Is the throttle linkage transmitting full travel to the throttle lever?	Yes: Check 32. No: Adjust or renew the throttle linkage as necessary.
32. Is the maximum speed stop screw setting correct?	Yes: Check 32. No: Adjust the engine maximum speed.

Compression test
The test should only be carried out using diesel test equipment. The figures quoted in 'GENERAL DATA' are for guidance only, and when considering the results of a compression test it is more important to have uniform readings between the cylinders, than the exact figures quoted in 'GENERAL DATA'.

A scatter of 138 kN/m^2 (20 lbf/in^2) is normal.

NOTE: Rocker clearances must be correct before carrying out a compression test.

GENERAL DATA

The engine specification may vary according to market requirements and from model to model. The manufacturers reserve the right to alter specifications with or without notice at any time. The policy of constant product improvement by the manufacturers may involve major or minor changes to the engine specification. Whilst every effort is made to ensure the accuracy of the particulars contained in this Handbook, no liability for inaccuracies or the consequences thereof can be accepted by the manufacturer or the supplier of the Handbook.

1·8 LITRE ENGINE. *For engine identification see page 27*

Engine	Type	18V
	Number of cylinders	4
	Bore	80·3 mm (3·16 in)
	Stroke	88·9 mm (3·5 in)
	Capacity	1799 cm³ (109·8 in³)
	Compression ratio:	
	Engines with early type camshaft	21·47 : 1
	Engines with later type camshaft	22·3 : 1
	Injection order	1, 3, 4, 2
	Valve rocker clearances (hot or cold):	
	Engines with early type camshaft	0·43 mm (0·017 in)
	Engines with later type camshaft	0·36 mm (0·014 in)
	Static injection timing	18° B.T.D.C.
	Maximum torque	107·1 Nm, 79 lbf ft, 10·9 kgf m
	Idling speed	650 to 700 rev/min
	Maximum governed light running speed (vehicle)	4,900 rev/min
	Typical compression pressures	2,750 to 2,888 kN/m² (400 to 420 lbf/in²) engine hot at 280 to 320 rev/min cranking speed
Fuel system	Fuel filter	C.A.V. type FS
	Fuel injection pump	C.A.V.—DPA3247F180
	Fuel injection nozzle	C.A.V.—BDN.OSPC.6651
	Fuel injection nozzle holder	C.A.V.—BKB.35SD.5188
	Nozzle opening pressure	135 Atmospheres
	Heater plugs	Champion type AG 32
	Fuel lift pump	A.C. mechanical
	Fuel lift pump setting	34·50 to 55·00 kN/m² (5 to 8 lbf/in²)
	Injector nut tightness	16 Nm, 12 lbf ft, 1·7 kgf m
Electrical equipment	Alternator	Lucas 16 ACR, 18 ACR or 17 ACR—M
	Starter	Lucas M45G pre-engaged
Capacities	Engine (including filter)	4·54 litres (8 pints)
	Filter only	0·43 litre (¾ pint)
Weight	Basic power unit	181·9 kg (400 lb)

General Data

1·5 LITRE ENGINE

Engine
- Type 15V
- Number of cylinders.. 4
- Bore .. .. 73·025 mm (2·875 in)
- Stroke .. .. 88·9 mm (3·5 in)
- Capacity .. .. 1489 cm³ (90·88 in³)
- Compression ratio .. .. .. 23 : 1
- Injection order 1, 3, 4, 2
- Valve rocker clearance (hot or cold) 0·38 mm (0·015 in)
- Static injection timing .. .. 22° B.T.D.C.
- Idling speed .. .. 550 to 600 rev/min
- Maximum governed light running speed (vehicle) .. .. .. 4,400 rev/min
- Typical compression pressures .. 3,300 to 3,438 kN/m² (480 to 500 lbf/in²) engine hot at 280 to 320 rev/min cranking speed

Fuel system
- Fuel filter .. .. C.A.V. type FS.5836020
- Fuel injection pump . .. C.A.V.—DPA.3246F857
- Fuel injection nozzle . .. C.A.V.—BDN.O.SPC.6389
- Fuel injection nozzle holder .. C.A.V.—BKB.35SD.5188
- Nozzle opening pressure . .. 135 Atmospheres
- Heater plugs .. .. KLG type GS103L or Champion AG32A
- Fuel lift pump .. . .. A.C. mechanical
- Fuel lift pump setting . .. 34·5 to 55·0 kN/m² (5 to 8 lbf/in²)
- Injector nut tightness . .. 16 Nm, 12 lbf ft, 1·7 kgf m

Electrical equipment
- Alternator . Lucas 16 ACR, 18 ACR or 17 ACR—M
- Starter . Lucas M45G pre-engaged

Capacities
- Engine (including filter) 4·66 litres (8¼ pints)
- Filter only .. .. 0·71 litre (1¼ pints)

Weight
- Basic power unit 186·4 kg (410 lb)

MAINTENANCE SUMMARY

This page contains a summary of the routine maintenance, and the periods at which it should be carried out, to maintain the efficient and economical running of the engine under normal operating and climatic conditions. Under abnormal conditions it may be necessary to adjust the recommended servicing intervals. The numbers quoted after an item refer to the page on which details of the individual operation will be found.

It is recommended that the 600 hour service be conducted once per year even if the engine has not been run for 600 hours.

Daily
Check/top up engine oil level (11)
Check/top up coolant in radiator

Every 150 hours
Change engine oil and oil filter (12)

Operation	Every 300 hours	Every 600 hours
Check/adjust drive belt tension (14)	x	x
Check/adjust valve clearances (13)	x	x
Renew main fuel filter element (10)	x	x
Change engine oil and filter element (12)	x	x
Test injectors for spray (10)		x
Remove heater plugs and clean carbon from each plug orifice in cylinder head (8)		x
Renew oil filler cap (11)		x
Clean fuel injection pump driving gear lubricator (1·5 Litre engine only) (12)		
Clean/renew air filter element (7)	x	x
Check governor settings (10)		x
Retorque cylinder head nuts (1·8 Litre engine only)	x	x

NOTE: More frequent air cleaner element servicing may be necessary in dirty/dusty conditions.

LUBRICATION

The lubrication systems of your new engine are filled with high quality oils.

You should always use a high quality multigrade oil of the correct viscosity range in the engine, during subsequent maintenance operations or when topping-up. The use of oils not to the recommended specification can lead to high oil and fuel consumption and ultimately to damage to the engine components.

Oil to the recommended specification contains additives which disperse the corrosive acids formed by combustion and also prevent the formation of sludge which can block oilways. **Additional oil additives should not be used.** Servicing intervals must be adhered to.

Engine Use a well-known brand of oil to MIL-L-46152 or MIL-L-2104B (A.P.I.–CC) quality, with a viscosity band spanning the temperature range of your locality.

Multigrade Oils Viscosity/Temperature Ranges

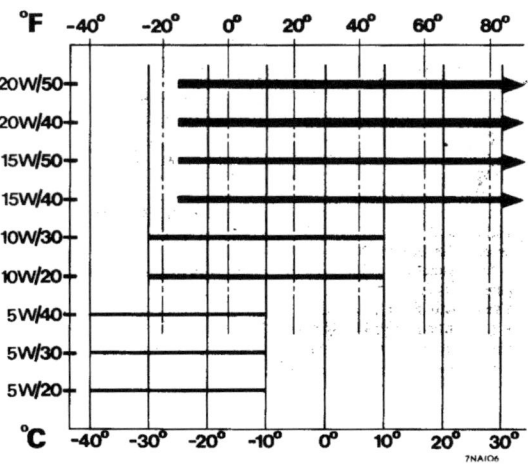

The use of monograde oil is possible, providing that it is of the correct viscosity for the ambient temperature of your locality. It should also be of the same quality MIL-L-46152 or MIL-L-2104B (A.P.I.-CC) as the preferred multigrade oils.

For sustained high speed operation or operation for long periods in a high ambient temperature, the use of a multigrade oil of the correct viscosity and quality is recommended.

Monograde Oils Viscosity/Temperature Ranges

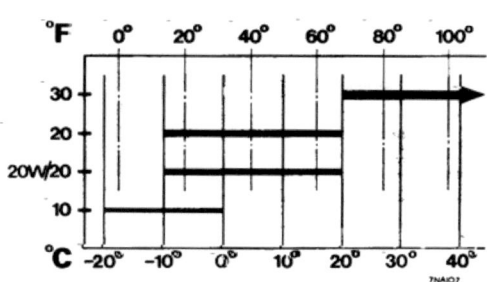

Lubrication

	FORECOURT OILS			FLEET OILS		
Minimum performance level	MIL-L-2104B (A.P.I.–CC) or MIL-L-46152					
Climatic Conditions	Temperatures above −10°C (10°F)	Temperatures −20°C (−5°F) to 10°C (50°F)	Temperatures below −10°C (10°F)	Temperatures above −10°C (10°F)	Temperatures −20°C (−5°F) to 10°C (50°F)	Temperatures below −10°C (10°F)
BP	BP Super Visco-Static 20W/50 BP Vanellus C3 Multi-grade BP Visco 2000*	BP Super Visco-Static 10W/30 or 10W/40*	BP Super Visco-Static 5W/20*	BP Vanellus M 20–50 BP Vanellus C3 Multigrade	BP Vanellus M 10W/30 or 10W/40*	BP Super Visco-Static 5W/20*
CASTROL	Castrol GTX 20W/50 Castrol GTX-2 15W/20	Castrolite 10W/30 or 10W/40 Castrol GTZ 10W/40 (Sweden)	Castrol Super GTX 5W/30 (Canada) Castrol GTZ 5W/40 (Finland)	Castrol Deusol RX Super 15W/40		
DUCKHAMS	Duckhams Q Motor Oil 20W/50	No grades in the U.K.		Fleetol Multi-V 20W/50 Fleetmaster	Fleetol Multilite 10W/30	
ESSO	Esso Uniflo 15W/50	Esso Uniflo 10W/40	Esso Uniflo 5W/40	Essolube HDX Plus 20W/50 Esso Uniflo 15W/50	Essolube HDX Plus 10W/30 Esso Uniflo 10W/40	Essolube MDX Plus 10W/30 Esso Uniflo 5W/40
MOBIL	Mobiloil Super 15W/50	Mobiloil SHC 10W/50	Mobiloil 1 5W/20 Mobiloil 5W/20	Mobil Delvac Super 15W/40 Delvac Special 20W/50	Mobil Delvac Special 10W/30	Mobiloil 5W/20
PETROFINA	Fina Supergrade Motor Oil 20W/50	Fina Supergrade Motor Oil 10W/40		Fina Delta Multigrade 20W/50	Fina Delta Multigrade 10W/30	
SHELL	Shell Super Motor Oil U.K. 20W/50 Europe 15W/30	Shell Super Motor Oil 10W/40 (Norway, Sweden, Canada) 10W/50 (Rest of Europe, U.S.A.)	Shell Super Motor Oil 5W/40 (Finland) 5W/30 (Canada)	Rotella SX Rotella TX 20W/40 Rotella SX 20W/30 (Sweden)	Rotella TX 10W/30 Rotella SX 10W/20 (Sweden)	Rotella TX 5W/20 (Finland, Canada)
TEXACO	Texaco URSA Oil LA 15W/40			Eurotex Motor oil HD 20W/50	Eurotex Motor oil HD 10W/30	

* Not available in the U.K.

SERVICE

Identification The engine number is stamped on the top face of the cylinder block on the right-hand side between number 2 and 3 cylinders.

1·5 Litre Engine

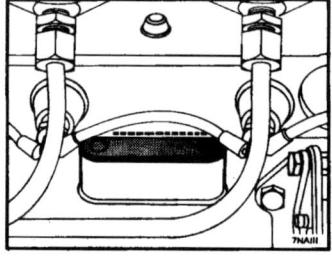

1·8 Litre Engine

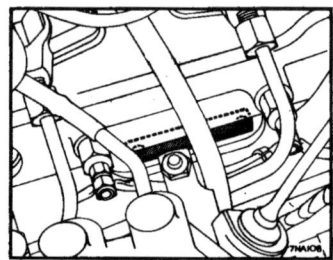

1·8 Litre Engine Identification

Engine with early type camshaft

Engine with later type camshaft

Service parts and accessories	Genuine LEYLAND and UNIPART parts and accessories are designed and tested for your engine and have the full backing of the Leyland Factory Warranty. **ONLY WHEN GENUINE LEYLAND AND UNIPART PARTS ARE USED CAN RESPONSIBILITY BE CONSIDERED UNDER THE TERMS OF THE WARRANTY.**

In accordance with the Company's policy of continuing improvement, new items are introduced regularly into the **UNIPART** range. **UNIPART** parts should be used when servicing or replacing parts on your engine.

Genuine Leyland and UNIPART parts and accessories are supplied in cartons and packs bearing either or both these symbols.

BMC (LEYLAND)

1,5 LITRE DIESEL ENGINE

REPAIR

OPERATION MANUAL

INTRODUCTION

This Manual is intended to assist the skilled mechanic in carrying out repairs and replacements in a minimum time. The information at the front of the book includes general data, recommended lubricants, and maintenance. Each major assembly or system is dealt with in a group, each group being sub-divided into parts for easy reference:

   A Description, Testing, and Adjusting (where applicable).
   B Removing and Refitting Components.
   C Overhauling.

An index is provided at the front of each group.

DISCLAIMER
(i) Purchasers are advised that the specification details set out in this Manual apply to a range of engines and not to any particular engine. For the specification of any particular engine Purchasers should consult their supplier.
(ii) The Manufacturers reserve the right to vary their specifications with or without notice, and at such times and in such manner as they think fit. Major as well as minor changes may be involved in accordance with the Manufacturer's policy of constant product improvement.
(iii) Whilst every effort is made to ensure the accuracy of the particulars contained in this Manual, neither the Manufacturer nor the supplier, by whom this Manual is supplied, shall in any circumstances be held liable for any inaccuracy or the consequences thereof.

REPAIRS AND REPLACEMENTS
When service parts are required it is essential that only genuine BL or Unipart replacements are used.
Attention is particularly drawn to the following points concerning repairs and the fitting of replacement parts and accessories:
Safety features embodied in the engine may be impaired if other than genuine parts are fitted. In certain territories, legislation prohibits the fitting of parts not to the engine manufacturer's specification. Torque wrench setting figures given in this Manual must be strictly adhered to. Locking devices, where specified, must be fitted. If the efficiency of a locking device is impaired during removal, it must be renewed. When purchasing accessories while travelling abroad ensure that the accessory and its fitted location conform to requirements existing in their country of origin. The engine warranty may be invalidated by the fitting of other than genuine BL or Unipart parts.
All BL or Unipart replacements have the full backing of the factory warranty.

SERVICE PARTS
Genuine BL or UNIPART Service Parts are designed and tested for your engine and have the full backing of the BL Cars Warranty. ONLY WHEN GENUINE BL or UNIPART SERVICE PARTS ARE USED CAN RESPONSIBILITY BE CONSIDERED UNDER THE TERMS OF THE WARRANTY. Genuine parts are supplied in cartons bearing one or both of these symbols:

ABBREVIATIONS

Across flats (bolt head size)	A.F.	Maximum	max.
After bottom dead centre	A.B.D.C.	Metres	m
After top dead centre	A.T.D.C.	Microfarad	mfd
Alternating current	a.c.	Millimetres	mm
Amperes	amp	Minimum	min.
Ampere-hour	Ah	Minus (of tolerance)	−
Atmospheres	Atm		
		Negative (electrical)	−
Before bottom dead centre	B.B.D.C.		
Before top dead centre	B.T.D.C.	Ohms	ohm or Ω
Bottom dead centre	B.D.C.	Ounces	oz
Brake horse-power	b.h.p.	Outside diameter	o.dia.
British Standards	B.S.		
		Pints (Imperial)	pt
Centigrade (Celsius)	C	Plus or minus	±
Centimetres	cm	Plus (of tolerance)	+
Centimetres of mercury	cmHg	Positive (electrical)	+
Cubic centimetres	cm^3	Pounds (force)	lbf
Cubic inches	in^3	Pounds (mass)	lb
		Pounds feet (torque)	lbf ft
		Pounds force per square inch	lbf/in^2
Degree, minute, second (angle)	°, ′, ″	Pounds inches (torque)	lbf in
Degree (temperature)	deg. or		
Diameter	dia.	Ratio	:
Direct current	d.c.	Revolutions per minute	rev/min
		Right-hand	R.H.
		Right-hand drive	R.H.D.
Fahrenheit	F		
Feet	ft	Society of Automobile Engineers	S.A.E.
		Specific gravity	sp. gr.
		Square centimetres	cm^2
Gallons (Imperial)	gal	Square inches	in^2
Grammes (mass)	g	Standard wire gauge	s.w.g.
Inches	in	Top dead centre	T.D.C.
Inches of mercury	InHg		
Internal diameter	i.dia	United Kingdom	U.K.
Kilogrammes (force)	kgf	Volts	V
Kilogrammes (mass)	kg		
Kilogramme centimetre (force)	kgf cm	Watts	W
Kilogramme metres (force)	kgf m		
Kilogrammes per square centimetre (force)	kgf/cm^2	Screw threads:	
Kilometres	km	British Association	B.A.
Kilonewtons per square metre	kN/m^2	British Standard Fine	B.S.F.
		British Standard Pipe	B.S.P.
		Metric (millimetres)	M
Left-hand		Unified Coarse	U.N.C.
Left-hand drive		Unified Fine	U.N.F.

GENERAL DATA

ENGINE

Engine type	15V
Number of cylinders	4
Bore	73·01 to 73·05 mm (2·8745 to 2·876 in)
Stroke	88·9 mm (3·5 in)
Capacity	1489 cm^3 (90·88 in^3)
Compression ratio	23 : 1
Firing order	1, 3, 4, 2
Idling speed	500 to 600 rev/min
Maximum governed speed	4,400 rev/min
Oil pressure:	
Idling	1·05 kgf/m^2 (15 lbf/in^2)
Normal running	3·52 kgf/m^2 (50 lbf/in^2)
Valve rocker clearance (cold)	0·38 mm (0·015 in)

FUEL SYSTEM

Injection pump	C.A.V. DPA. 3246F857
Injectors	C.A.V.
Nozzle	BDN.0.SCP.5389
Nozzle holder	BKB.35.SD.S188
Nozzle opening pressure	135 atmospheres
Lift pump	A.C. mechanical, U-type
Main filter	C.A.V. FS.5836020
Lift pump static pressure (no delivery)	0·35 to 0·56 kgf/cm^2 (5 to 8 lbf/in^2)

CAPACITIES

Engine oil (including filter)	4·7 litres (8·25 imp. pints)

TORQUE WRENCH SETTINGS

ENGINE

Big-end bolts	4·84 kgf m (35 lbf ft)
Cylinder head nuts	9·8 kgf m (71 lbf ft)
Flywheel bolts	5·1 kgf m (37 lbf ft)
Fuel injector securing nuts ..	1·7 kgf m (12 lbf ft)
Main bearing nuts	10·4 kgf m (75 lbf ft)
Manifold nuts	2·1 kgf m (15 lbf ft)
Rear distance piece bolts: $\frac{7}{16}$ in	2·8 kgf m (20 lbf ft)
$\frac{1}{2}$ in	4·1 kgf m (30 lbf ft)
Rocker bracket nuts..	3·4 kgf m (25 lbf ft)
Water pump bolts ..	2·3 kgf m (17 lbf ft)

INJECTION PUMP

Advance unit cap nut	1·5 kgf m (130 lbf in)
Advance unit cap nut stud	0·69 kgf m (60 lbf in)
Advance unit spring cap and end-plug	2·88 kgf m (250 lbf in)
Cam ring advance screw	5·02 kgf m (450 lbf in)
Drive plate screws:	
Direct torque	1·85 kgf m (160 lbf in)
Indirect torque (using tool 18G 655 A)	1·62 kgf m (140 lbf in)
End plate studs	0·52 kgf m (45 lbf in)
Fuel inlet connection	5·02 kgf m (450 lbf in)
Governor housing securing screws ..	0·46 kgf m (40 lbf in)
High-pressure connections	3·12 kgf m (270 lbf in)
Hydraulic head locating bolt	4·03 kgf m (350 lbf in)
Hydraulic head locating screws	1·96 kgf m (170 lbf in)
Rotor end-plug	0·52 kgf m (28 lbf in)
Transfer pump rotor	0·75 kgf m (65 lbf in)

INJECTORS

Nozzle nut	6·91 kgf m (50 lbf ft)

Torque Wrench Settings 2

50D

DIESEL ENGINE

TRANSVERSE SECTION

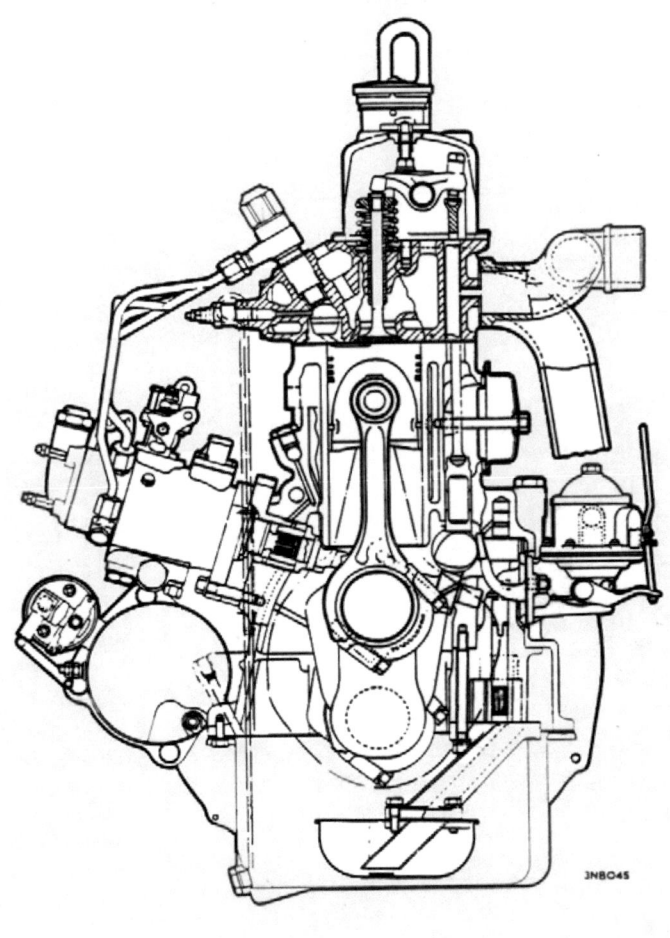

DIESEL ENGINE **50D**

LONGITUDINAL SECTION

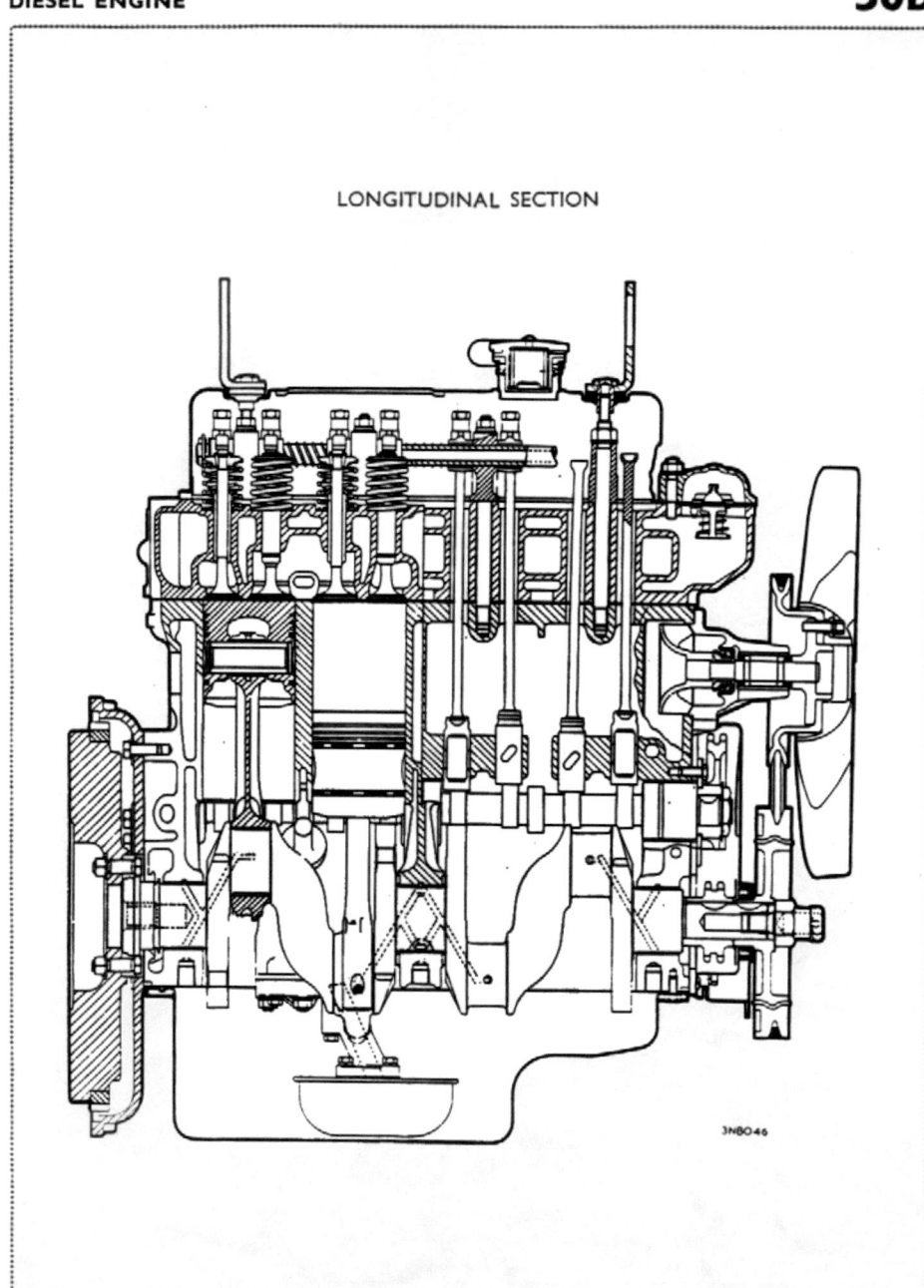

3NB046

DIESEL ENGINE

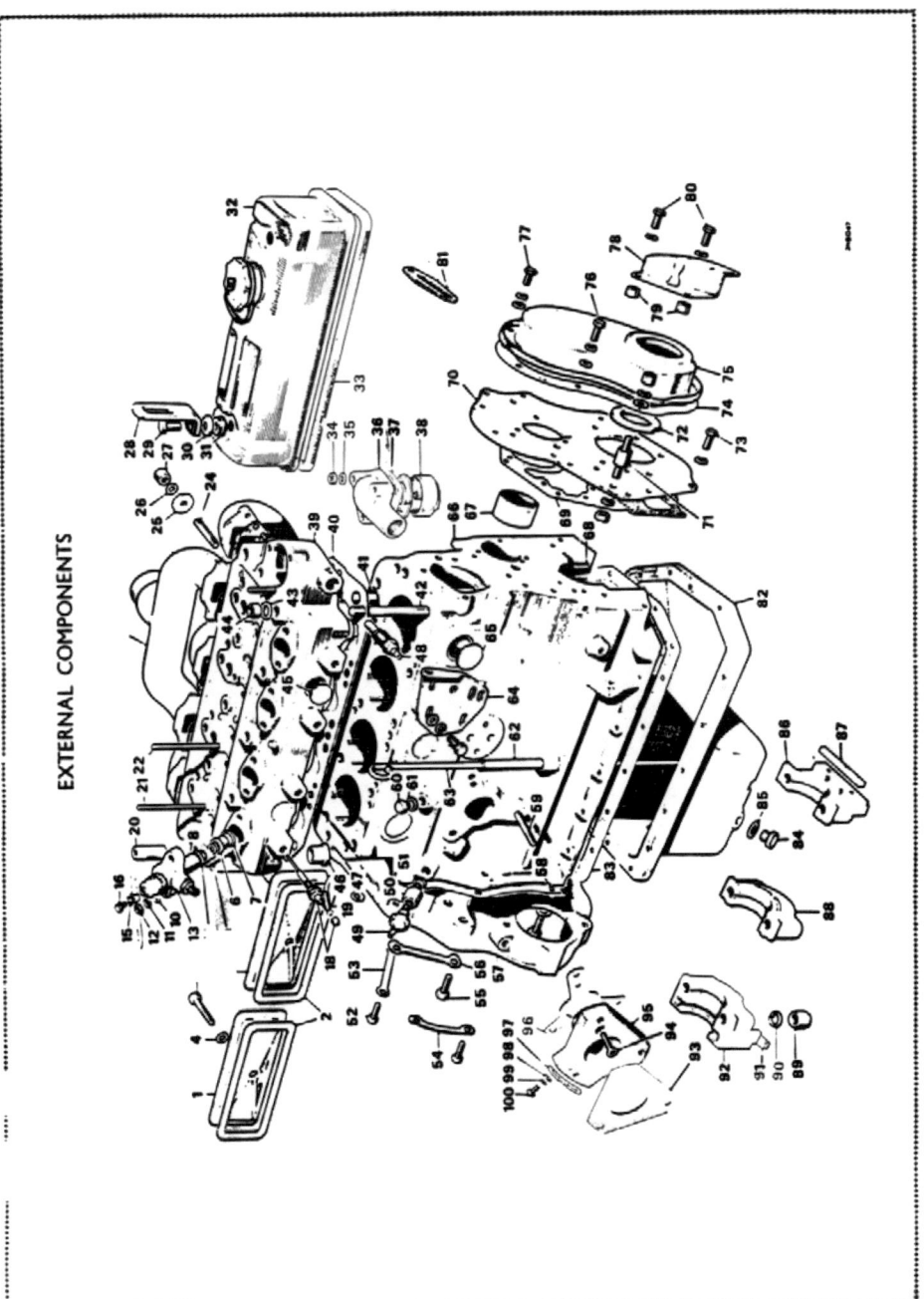

EXTERNAL COMPONENTS

DIESEL ENGINE

50D

KEY TO EXTERNAL COMPONENTS

No.	Description
1.	Tappet side cover—rear
2.	Gasket for side cover
3.	Bolt for side cover
4.	Washer for bolt
5.	Tappet side cover—front
6.	Heat shield
7.	Joint washer for heat shield
8.	Atomizer seal washer
9.	Stud for injector
10.	Washer for nut
11.	Spring washer for nut
12.	Nut for injector stud
13.	Injector
14.	Joint washer for injector
15.	Washer for banjo bolt
16.	Banjo bolt
17.	Leak-off pipe
18.	Heater plug
19.	Cable for heater plug
20.	Pedestal for fuel filter bracket
21.	Long stud for rocker bracket
22.	Short stud for rocker bracket
23.	Inlet manifold
24.	Stud for manifold
25.	Large washer for stud
26.	Washer for stud
27.	Nut for stud
28.	Engine sling bracket
29.	Cap nut for rocker cover
30.	Cup washer
31.	Rubber bush
32.	Rocker cover
33.	Gasket for rocker cover
34.	Nut for water outlet elbow

No.	Description
35.	Washer for nut
36.	Water outlet elbow
37.	Gasket for elbow
38.	Thermostat
39.	Cylinder head
40.	Gasket for cylinder head
41.	Cylinder head stud (long)
42.	Cylinder head stud (short)
43.	Washer for stud
44.	Nut for stud
45.	Core plug
46.	Combustion chamber insert
47.	Ball for insert (if fitted)
48.	Thermal transmitter
49.	Oil pressure switch
50.	Adaptor for switch
51.	Seal washer for adaptor
52.	Screw for gearbox distance piece
53.	Lock washer for screw
54.	Lock washer for screw
55.	Screw for gearbox distance piece
56.	Lock washer for screw
57.	Gearbox distance piece
58.	Gasket for distance piece
59.	Stud for injector pump
60.	Plug for oil gallery
61.	Washer for plug
62.	Guide tube for dipstick
63.	Oil dipstick
64.	Bracket for alternator
65.	Core plug
66.	Cylinder block
67.	Camshaft bearing liner

No.	Description
68.	Stud for main bearing cap
69.	Gasket for engine front plate
70.	Engine front plate
71.	Pillar for alternator adjusting link
72.	Crankshaft oil seal
73.	Screw for front plate
74.	Gasket for front cover
75.	Front cover
76.	Screw for front cover and front plate
77.	Screw for front cover
78.	Timing plate
79.	Distance piece
80.	Screw for timing plate
81.	Adjusting link for alternator
82.	Oil sump
83.	Gasket for sump
84.	Drain plug for sump
85.	Washer for drain plug
86.	Front main bearing cap
87.	Joint for main bearing cap
88.	Centre main bearing cap
89.	Nut for main bearing cap
90.	Washer for nut
91.	Joint for rear main bearing cap
92.	Rear main bearing cap
93.	Gasket for injection pump
94.	Countersunk screw for hub
95.	Hub for injection pump
96.	Gasket for hub
97.	Timing pointer
98.	Plain washer
99.	Spring washer
100.	Screw for timing pointer

50D

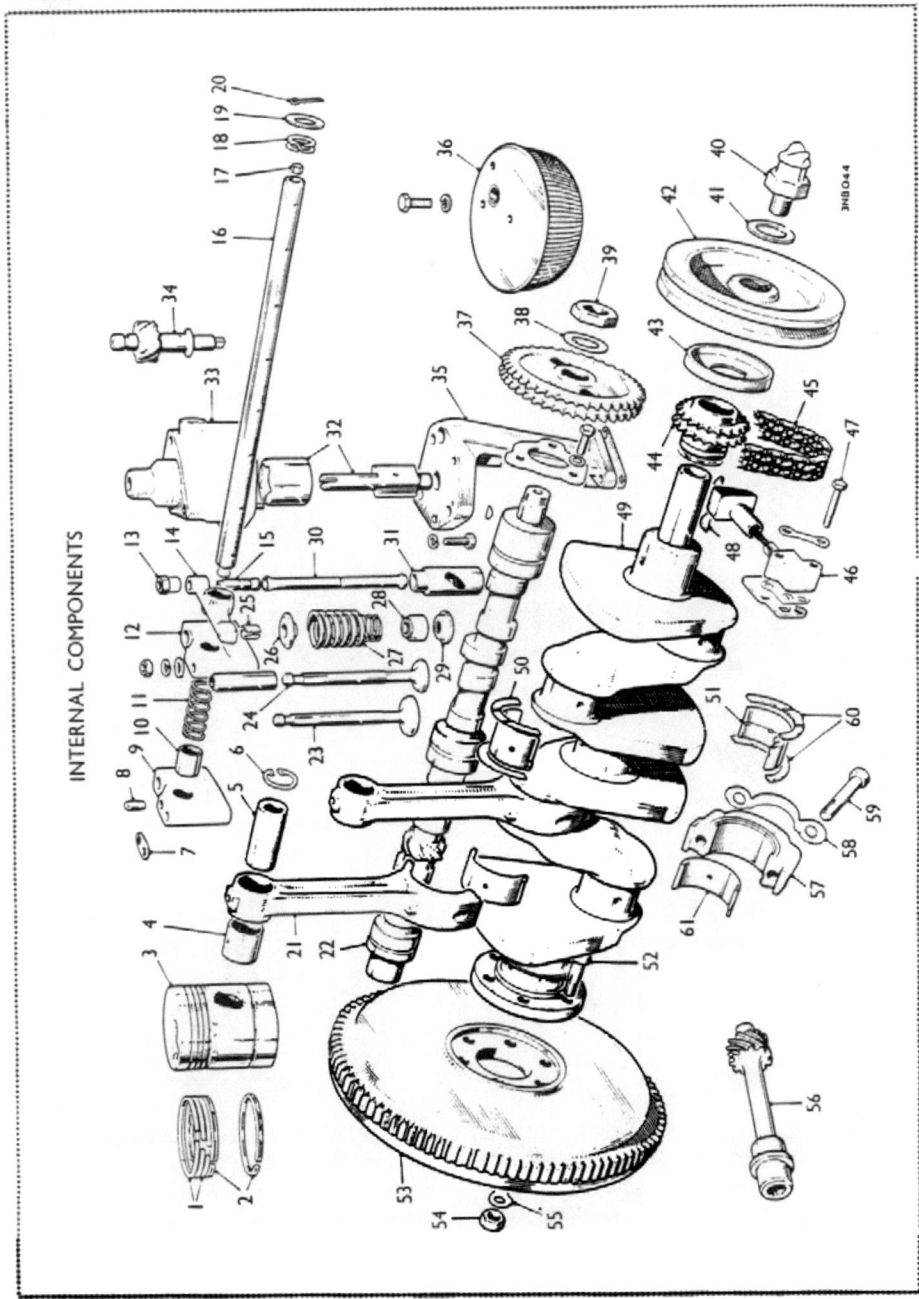

INTERNAL COMPONENTS

DIESEL ENGINE 50D

KEY TO INTERNAL COMPONENTS

No.	Description
1.	Piston rings—compression
2.	Piston rings—oil scraper
3.	Piston
4.	Small end bush
5.	Gudgeon pin
6.	Circlip for gudgeon pin
7.	Locking plate for locating screw
8.	Rocker shaft locating screw
9.	Rocker bracket (tapped)
10.	Bush for rocker
11.	Spacing spring for rocker
12.	Rocker bracket (plain)
13.	Locknut for adjusting screw
14.	Valve rocker
15.	Adjusting screw for rocker
16.	Rocker shaft
17.	Plug for rocker shaft
18.	Double-coil spring washer
19.	Rocker shaft washer
20.	Split pin
21.	Connecting rod
22.	Camshaft
23.	Inlet valve
24.	Exhaust valve
25.	Valve cotters
26.	Valve spring cap
27.	Valve springs
28.	Valve stem oil seal
29.	Valve spring bottom collar
30.	Push-rod
31.	Tappet
32.	Oil pump rotor assembly
33.	Oil pump body
34.	Oil pump driving spindle
35.	Oil pump cover
36.	Oil strainer
37.	Camshaft chain wheel
38.	Lock washer for nut
39.	Camshaft nut
40.	Starting nut
41.	Lock washer for nut
42.	Crankshaft pulley
43.	Crankshaft oil thrower
44.	Crankshaft chain wheel
45.	Timing chain
46.	Chain tensioner
47.	Bolt for chain tensioner
48.	Key for crankshaft
49.	Crankshaft
50.	Crankshaft thrust washer (upper)
51.	Main bearing shell
52.	Flywheel bolt
53.	Flywheel
54.	Nut for flywheel bolt
55.	Lock washer for nut
56.	Injection pump driving spindle
57.	Connecting rod cap
58.	Lock washer for bolt
59.	Bolt for connecting rod cap
60.	Crankshaft thrust washer (lower)
61.	Big-end bearing shell

50D

DIESEL ENGINE

Section B1

ENGINE (with gearbox)

Removing

1. Drain the cooling system.
2. Disconnect the battery.
3. Remove engine cover.
4. Remove the radiator.
5. Remove the breather pipe from the air cleaner.
6. Slacken the clip retaining the air cleaner assembly to the inlet manifold and detach the air cleaner assembly.
7. Disconnect the exhaust pipe from the exhaust manifold.
8. Disconnect the fuel feed pipe from the fuel lift pump.
9. Disconnect the electrical leads from the thermal transmitter, oil pressure switch, heater plugs, alternator and starter.
10. Disconnect the throttle and stop control cable from the fuel injection pump. See Fig. 1.
11. Remove the nuts securing the cable abutment bracket to the fuel injection pump and detach the bracket and cables from the pump (Fig. 1).
12. Disconnect the fuel leak-off pipe from its union on the top of the fuel filter.
13. Support the engine with an overhead crane or hoist, with the point of lift towards the rear of the engine.
14. Disconnect the engine earth cable from the body.
15. Disconnect the exhaust pipe front clip from its bracket.
16. Remove the bolts securing engine mounting.
17. Remove the screws and bolts securing the flywheel housing.
18. Lift the engine clear of the frame.

Refitting

19. Reverse the procedure in 1 to 18, noting:
    a. Bleed the fuel system.

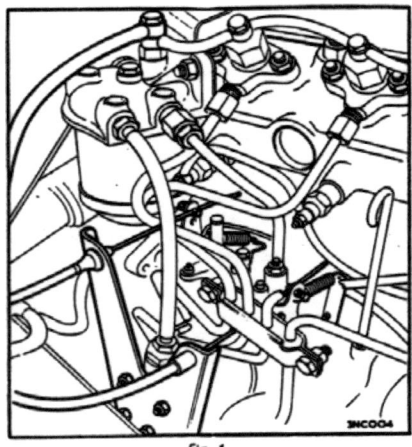

Fig. 1

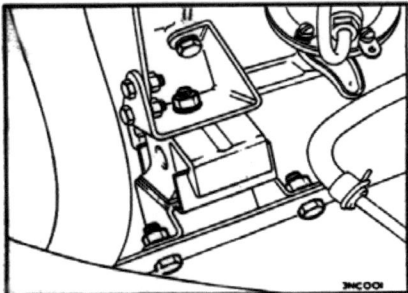

Fig. 2

DIESEL ENGINE

50D

Section B2

VALVE ROCKER SHAFT AND TAPPETS

Removing
1. Disconnect the battery and drain the cooling system.
2. Remove the air cleaner.
3. Remove the valve rocker cover.
4. Slacken the cylinder head nuts in the order shown in Fig. 1, using tool 18G 694.
5. Release the rocker brackets from the cylinder head and lift off the rocker shaft assembly.
6. Withdraw the push-rods, storing them in the correct order for replacement.
7. Remove the cylinder side covers.
8. Lift out the tappets, storing them in the correct order for replacement.

Refitting
9. Reverse the procedure in 1 to 8, noting:
   a. Refer to Data for torque wrench settings.
   b. Tighten the cylinder head nuts in the order shown in Fig. 1.
   c. Adjust the valve rocker clearances.

Data
Torque wrench setting for cylinder head nuts .. 918 kgf m (71 lbf ft)

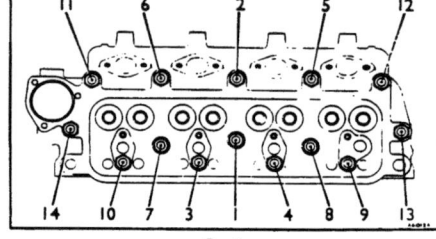

Fig. 1

Section B3

CYLINDER HEAD

Removing
1. Disconnect the battery and drain the cooling system.
2. Remove the air cleaner.
3. Remove the valve rocker cover and rocker shaft.
4. Withdraw the push-rods.
5. Release the leak-off pipe from its union on the fuel filter head.
6. Remove the high-pressure fuel feed pipes and the injection pump feed and return pipes.
7. Remove the main fuel filter and its mounting bracket.

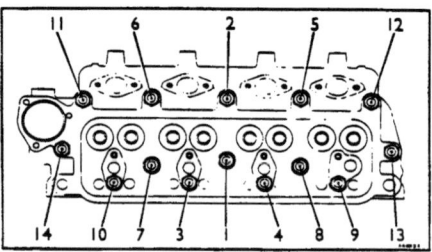

Fig. 1

40

50D

DIESEL ENGINE

8. Disconnect the electrical lead from the heater plugs and the thermal transmitter.
9. Remove the clamp and release the exhaust pipe from the exhaust manifold.
10. Remove the exhaust and inlet manifold from the cylinder head.
11. Disconnect the top water hose.
12. Remove the cylinder head nuts and lift off the cylinder head.
    NOTE: Should combustion chamber inserts drop when the cylinder head is lifted they must be refitted in their original positions because the cylinder head face is machined with the inserts installed.

Refitting

13. Reverse the procedure in 1 to 12, noting:
    a. Refer to Data for torque wrench settings.
    b. Tighten the cylinder head nuts in the order shown in Fig. 1, using tool 18G 694.
    c. Adjust the valve rocker clearances.
    d. Bleed the fuel system.

Data

Torque wrench setting for cylinder head nuts   9·8 kgf m (71 lbf ft)

Section B4

TIMING CHAIN TENSIONER

Removing

1. Disconnect the battery and drain the cooling system.
2. Remove the radiator.
3. Slacken the alternator mounting bolts and remove the driving belt.
4. Remove the fan blades and pulley.
5. Remove the crankshaft nut, using tool 18G 98 A, and withdraw the crankshaft pulley.
6. Remove the timing chain cover.
7. Unlock and remove the chain tensioner securing screws.
8. Carefully prise the tensioner assembly out of its register in the front engine plate. The slipper head is under spring tension.
9. Allow the spring loading against the slipper head to relax and withdraw the slipper head, spring and inner cylinder from the tensioner body.

Refitting

10. Refit the inner cylinder and spring into the cylinder of the slipper head so that the serrated helical slot in the inner cylinder engages with the peg in the slipper cylinder.
11. Turn the inner cylinder clockwise against spring tension until the lower serration in the slot engages with the peg and retains the inner cylinder in the slipper cylinder.
12. Refit the assembly in the tensioner body and fit to the engine.
13. Press the slipper head into the body against the spring and release it smartly to disengage the inner cylinder and allow the spring to re-assert itself fully against the slipper head and timing chain.

Data

Maximum permissible body bore ovality ..   0·076 mm (0·003 in)

Section B5

TIMING CHAIN, CHAIN WHEELS AND CHAIN TENSIONER

Removing

1. Disconnect the battery and drain the cooling system.
2. Remove the radiator.
3. Slacken the alternator mounting bolts and remove the driving belt.
4. Remove the fan blades and pulley.
5. Remove the crankshaft nut, using tool 18G 98 A, and withdraw the crankshaft pulley.
6. Remove the timing gear cover.
7. Remove the oil thrower from the crankshaft.

DIESEL ENGINE 50D

8. Unlock and remove the camshaft nut, using tool 18G 98 A.
9. Position the chain wheel timing marks as shown in Fig. 1.
10. Remove the chain tensioner.
11. Draw the two chain wheels off their shafts complete with chain.

Refitting

12. Reverse the procedure in 1 to 11, noting:
    a. Check the chain wheel alignment (see Data).
    b. Assemble the chain wheels and chain on the shafts with the timing marks as shown in Fig. 1.
    c. Ensure the crankshaft front oil seal in the cover is serviceable. Renew the seal if necessary, using tools 18G 134 and 18G 134 BD.
    d. Centralize the timing gear cover with the crankshaft using tool 18G 1046.

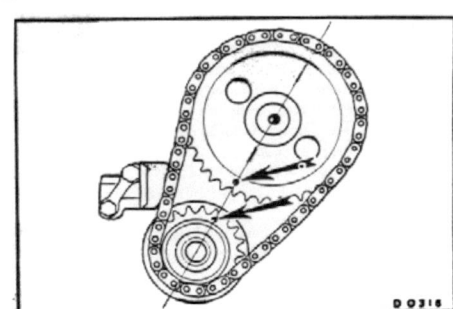

Fig. 1

Data

Crankshaft chain wheel face aligned rearwards of camshaft
 chain wheel face by .. ..   0·127 mm (0·005 in)
 Method of adjustment .. ..   Shims behind crankshaft chain wheel

---

Section B6

FUEL INJECTION PUMP DRIVING SPINDLE

Removing

1. Disconnect the battery.
2. Remove the fuel injection pump.
3. Remove the countersunk screw and withdraw the fuel injection pump hub from the crankcase.
4. Withdraw the injection pump driving spindle, rotating it clockwise to disengage it from the camshaft gear.

Refitting

5. Reverse the procedure in 1 to 4, noting:
    a. Ensure that, when the driving spindle is fully home, its master spline is in the 5 o'clock position with No. 1 piston at 22° B.T.D.C. on compression stroke.
    b. When refitting the fuel injection pump, position it as described in 'MAINTENANCE'.
    c. Bleed the fuel system (see 'MAINTENANCE').
    d. Adjust the governed speed (see 'MAINTENANCE')'

Section B7

OIL PUMP AND DRIVING SPINDLE

Removing

1. Disconnect the battery and drain the oil from the sump.
2. Remove the starter motor.
3. Remove the sump.
4. Disconnect the oil suction pipe from the oil pump.
5. Remove the oil strainer assembly.
6. Remove the securing nuts and withdraw the oil pump.
7. Remove the fuel injection pump.
8. Remove the countersunk screw and withdraw the fuel injection pump hub from the crankcase.

BS

50D

DIESEL ENGINE

9. Withdraw the fuel injection pump drive spindle.
10. Withdraw the oil pump driving spindle.

Refitting
11. Reverse the procedure in 1 to 10, noting:
    a. Ensure that, when the injection pump driving spindle is fully home, its master spline is in the 5 o'clock position with No. 1 piston at 22° B.T.D.C. on compression stroke.
    b. When refitting the fuel injection pump, position it as described in 'MAINTENANCE'.
    c. Bleed the fuel system (see 'MAINTENANCE').
    d. Adjust the governed speed (see 'MAINTENANCE').

Section B8

CAMSHAFT AND FRONT PLATE

Removing
1. Disconnect the battery and drain the cooling system.
2. Remove the radiator.
3. Slacken the alternator mounting bolts and remove the driving belt.
4. Remove the fan blades and fan pulley.
5. Remove the crankshaft nut, using tool 18G 98 A, and withdraw the crankshaft pulley.
6. Remove the timing gear cover and the crankshaft oil thrower.
7. Unlock and remove the camshaft nut, using tool 18G 98 A.
8. Position the gear wheel timing marks as shown in Fig. 1.
9. Remove the chain tensioner.
10. Draw both chain wheels off their shafts complete with chain.
11. Remove the camshaft locating plate.
    If the front plate is not to be removed omit 12, 13, and 15.
12. Support the engine with an overhead crane or hoist.
13. Remove the bolts retaining the front engine mountings to the body.
14. Remove the bolts retaining the engine mounting brackets to the front plate and crankcase and detach the engine mounting assemblies (Fig. 2).
15. Remove the front plate.
16. Remove the valve rocker cover and the rocker shaft assembly.
17. Withdraw the push-rods. Retain them in their correct order as fitted.
18. Remove the fuel injection pump.
19. Remove the injection pump hub.

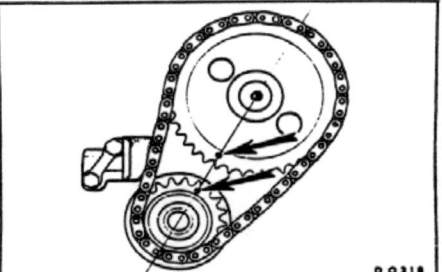

Fig. 1

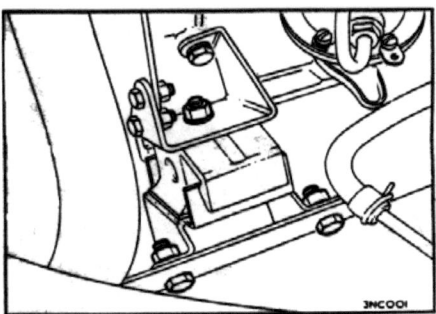

Fig. 2

DIESEL ENGINE 50D

20. Remove the injection pump driving spindle.
21. Remove the fuel lift pump.
22. Remove the cylinder side covers and lift out the tappets. Retain the tappets in their fitted order.
23. Remove the starter motor.
24. Drain the oil from the sump, and remove the sump.
25. Remove the oil pump and driving spindle.
26. Withdraw the camshaft.

Refitting

27. Reverse the procedure in 1 to 26, noting:
    a. Check the camshaft end float against the figure given in Data.
    b. Check the chain wheel alignment against the figure given in Data.
    c. Assemble the chain wheels and chain to the shafts with the timing marks as shown in Fig. 1.
    d. If necessary, renew the oil seal in the timing gear cover, using tools 18G 134 and 18G 134 BD.
    e. Centralize the cover with the crankshaft, using tool 18G 1046.
    f. When the injection pump driving spindle is fully home check that the master spline is in the 5 o'clock position with No. 1 piston at 22° B.T.D.C. on compression stroke.

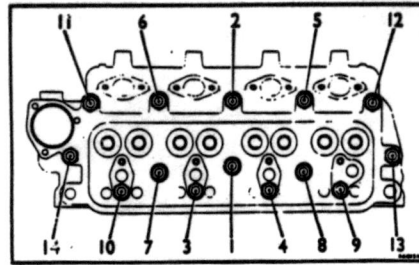

Fig. 3

g. When refitting the fuel injection pump, position it as described in 'MAINTENANCE'.
h. Refer to Data for torque wrench settings.
j. Tighten the cylinder head nuts in the order shown in Fig. 3.
k. Adjust the valve rocker clearances.
l. Bleed the fuel system.
m. Adjust the governed speed (see 'MAINTENANCE').

Data

Camshaft end-float	0·076 to 0·178 mm (0·003 to 0·007 in)
Crankshaft chain wheel face aligned rearwards of camshaft chain wheel face by	0·127 mm (0·005 in)
Method of adjustment	Shims behind crankshaft chain wheel
Torque wrench setting for rocker bracket nuts	3·5 kgf m (25 lbf ft)

50D

DIESEL ENGINE

Section B9

CONNECTING RODS AND PISTONS

Removing

1. Disconnect the battery.
2. Drain the cooling system.
3. Remove the air cleaner and breather hose.
4. Remove the rocker shaft and withdraw the push-rods.
5. Release the leak-off pipe from its union on the fuel filter head.
6. Remove the high pressure fuel feed pipes and the injection pump feed and return pipes.
7. Remove the main fuel filter and its mounting bracket.
8. Disconnect the electrical lead from the heater plugs and the thermal transmitter.
9. Remove the clamp and release the exhaust pipe from the exhaust manifold.
10. Remove the exhaust and inlet manifold from the cylinder head.
11. Disconnect the top water hose from the cylinder head.
12. Remove the cylinder head nuts and lift off the cylinder head.
    NOTE: The combustion chamber inserts are a loose fit in the cylinder head. They must be refitted in their original positions because the cylinder head face is machined with the inserts installed.
13. Drain the oil and remove the sump.
14. Remove the oil pump and strainer.
15. Remove the big-end bearing caps.
16. Withdraw the connecting rods and pistons upwards.

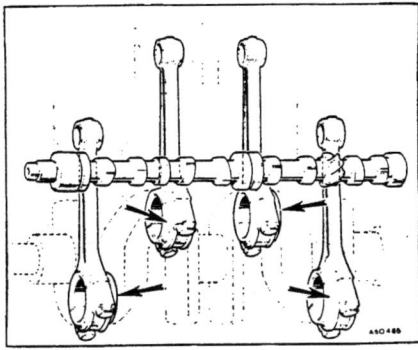

Fig. 1

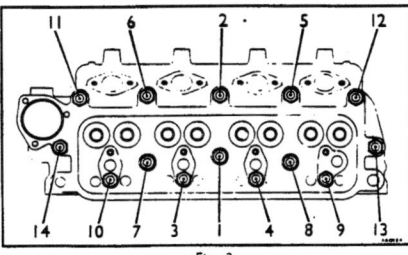

Fig. 2

Refitting

17. Reverse the procedure in 1 to 16, noting:
    a. Refer to Data for torque wrench settings.
    b. Fit the connecting rods with their offsets as shown in Fig. 1, using tool 18G 55 A to compress the piston rings.
    c. Tighten the cylinder head nuts in the order shown in Fig. 2, using tool 18G 694.
    d. Adjust the valve rocker clearance.
    e. Bleed the fuel system.

Data

Torque wrench settings:
Big-end bearing cap bolts	4·84 kgf m (35 lbf ft)
Cylinder head nuts	9·8 kgf m (71 lbf ft)
Manifold nuts	2·1 kgf m (15 lbf ft)
Rocker bracket nuts	3·4 kgf m (25 lbf ft)

DIESEL ENGINE 50D

Section B10

FLYWHEEL

Removing
1. Remove the engine.
2. Mark the clutch assembly and the flywheel for re-assembly.
3. Remove the drive assembly.
4. Unlock and remove the flywheel retaining nuts and lock washers.
5. Mark the flywheel and crankshaft flange for reassembly, or set the engine with No. 1 piston at T.D.C. and the flywheel with its mark 1/4 at the top.
6. Remove the flywheel.

Refitting
7. Reverse the procedure in 1 to 6, noting:
   a. Bleed the fuel system.

Data
Torque wrench setting for flywheel bolts   5·1 kgf m (37 lbf ft)

Section B11

CRANKSHAFT

Removing
1. Drain the sump.
2. Remove the engine (see Section 1).
3. Slacken the alternator mounting bolts and remove the driving belt.
4. Remove the fan blades and pulley.
5. Remove the crankshaft nut, using tool 18G 98 A.
6. Withdraw the crankshaft pulley.
7. Remove the timing cover.
8. Remove the oil thrower from the crankshaft.
9. Remove the camshaft nut, using tool 18G 98 A.
10. Remove the chain tensioner, noting that the slipper head is under spring tension.
11. Draw both chain wheels and chain off their shafts.
12. Remove the camshaft locating plate.
13. Remove the front engine plate.
14. Remove the flywheel and starter motor.
15. Remove the flywheel housing.
16. Remove the sump.
17. Remove the oil pump and strainer.
18. Remove the big-end bearing caps.
19. Remove the main bearing caps, using tools 18G 284 and 18G 284 A.
20. Lift out the crankshaft and collect the main bearing and thrust washer halves.

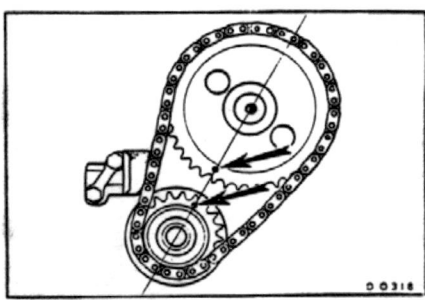

Fig.

Refitting
21. Reverse the procedure in 1 to 20, noting:
   a. Check the crankshaft end-float against the figure given in Data.
   b. Refer to Data for torque wrench settings.
   c. Fit the flywheel so that its 1/4 mark is at the top when Nos. 1 and 4 pistons are at top dead centre.

50D
DIESEL ENGINE

    d. Checks the timing chain wheel alignment. See Data.
    e. Assemble the chain and chain wheels with the timing marks as shown in Fig. 1.
    f. If necessary, renew the timing cover oil seal using tools 18G 134 and 18G 134 BD.
    g. Centralize the timing cover with the crankshaft using tool 18G 1046.
    h. Bleed the fuel system.

Data
Crankshaft chain wheel face aligned rearwards of camshaft
    chain wheel face by .. .. 0·127 mm (0·005 in)
    Method of adjustment .. .. Shims behind crankshaft chain wheel
Torque wrench settings:
    Big-end bolts .. .. 4·84 kgf m (35 lbf ft)
    Main bearing nuts .. .. 10·4 kgf m (75 lbf ft)

50D DIESEL ENGINE

Section C1

VALVE ROCKER SHAFT AND TAPPETS

Valve rockers

1. Remove the shaft locating screw from the rear rocker bracket.
2. Withdraw the split pins from the shaft ends.
3. Slide the components off the rocker shaft.
4. Unscrew the plug from the front end of the shaft to clean the shaft internally.
5. Renew worn rocker bushes, using tool 18G 226 as shown in Fig. 1.
    a. Drill the bushes to coincide with the oilways in the rockers.
    b. Position the bushes in the rockers as shown in Fig. 2.
6. Burnish-ream the bushes to the dimension given in Data.
7. Fit the rear rocker bracket to the shaft and position it with the locating screw.
8. Fit the remaining components to the shaft in the positions shown in Fig. 3.
9. Worn tappet bores may be cleaned up by fine-finish machining to suit oversize tappets (see Data).

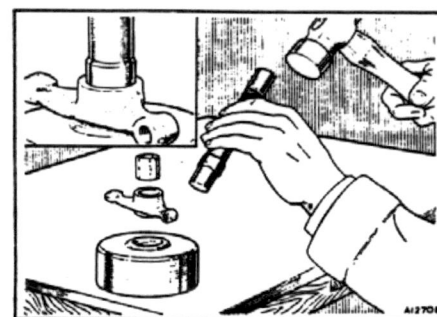

Fig. 1

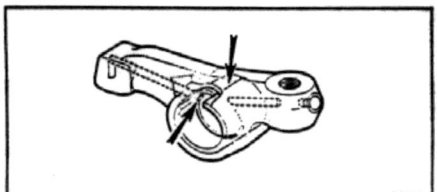

Fig. 2

Fig. 3

Data

Bush bore reamed diameter	15·888 to 15·9 mm (0·6255 to 0·626 in)
Tappet diameter	20·65 to 20·618 mm (0·81125 to 0·81175 in)
Tappet oversizes	0·254 and 0·508 mm (0·010 and 0·020 in)
Clearance in crankcase	0·013 to 0·051 mm (0·0005 to 0·002 in)

DIESEL ENGINE

50D

Section C2

CYLINDER HEAD

1. Detach the spring clips from the valve cotters.
2. Remove the valves and their components, using tool 18G 45.
3. Renew the valve springs if, when compressed under the same load as a new spring, they show more than $\frac{1}{16}$ in more compression compared with a new spring.
4. If the valve guides are worn, drive them out through the upper face of the cylinder head. Fit new valve guides through the ports and drive them in to the position shown in Fig. 2.
5. Check the cylinder head face for flatness. Reface the surface if necessary to the dimensions given in Data.
6. If necessary, regrind the valves to the angle given in Data, and reface the valve seats with the tools listed in 'SERVICE TOOLS'.
7. Lap the valves onto their seats, using tool 18G 29.
8. Check the valve head stand-down (see Data). If stand-down is excessive, even with a new valve fitted, machine the cylinder head (see Data) and fit valve seat inserts. Inserts should also be fitted if normal refacing will not restore the seats.
9. Renew the valve stem oil seals, and reassemble the valve components to the cylinder head as shown in Fig. 1.

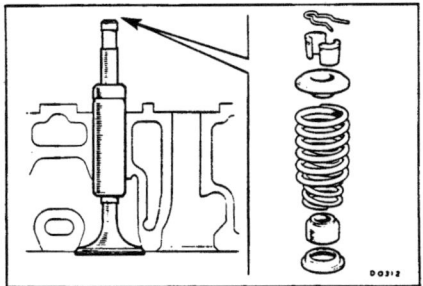

Fig. 1

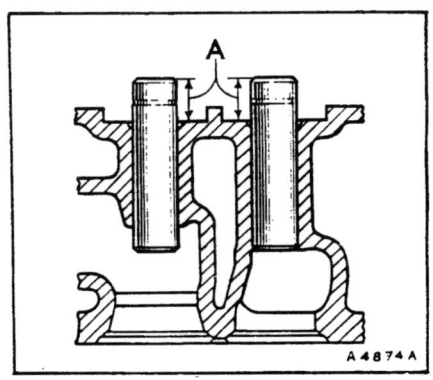

Fig. 2

Data

Cylinder head skimming allowance   0·38 mm (0·015 in) provided the finished cylinder head depth is not less than 80·19 mm (3·157 in)

Valve seating face angle $44\frac{1}{2}°$

Valve head stand-down   0·508 to 0·762 mm (0·020 to 0·030 in)

Section C3

TIMING CHAIN TENSIONER

1. If ovality near the mouth of the tensioner body bore exceeds 0·076 mm (0·003 in) renew the complete chain tensioner.
2. If the slipper head is worn, renew the slipper head and cylinder assembly.

50D DIESEL ENGINE

Section C4

OIL PRESSURE RELIEF VALVE

1. Unscrew the cap nut shown in Fig. 1 and withdraw the relief valve spring.
2. Remove the valve cup, using tool 18G 69.
3. If the valve cup to seat contact is unsatisfactory, lap the valve cup onto its seat with tool 18G 69.
4. Renew the valve spring if free length is less than 72·64 mm (2·86 in).
5. Reassemble the components to the crankcase.

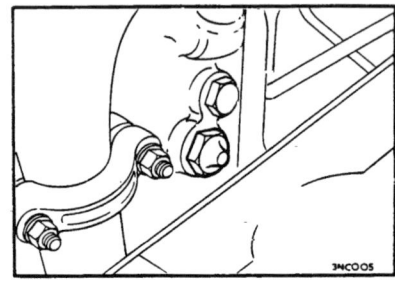

Fig. 1

Section C5

INJECTION PUMP DRIVING GEAR LUBRICATOR AND FILTER

1. Unscrew the lubricator from the crankcase and clean it thoroughly.
2. Unscrew the lubricator filter from the crankcase and clean it thoroughly.
3. Refit the filter and lubricator.

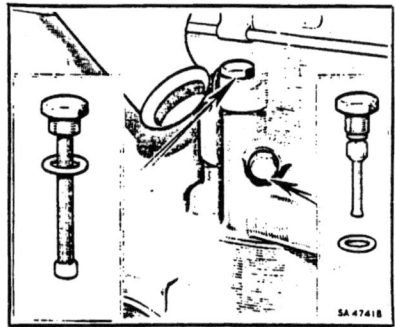

Fig. 1

DIESEL ENGINE 50D

Section C6

OIL PUMP

1. Remove the pump cover.
2. Check the rotor end-float against the figure in Data. Excessive end-float can be corrected by lapping the pump body face.
3. Check the diametrical clearance between the outer rotor and the pump body against the figure in Data. Renew the rotors, or pump body, or both, as necessary to correct excessive clearance.
4. Check the rotor lobe clearance (in two positions) against the figure in Data. Renew the rotors if clearance is excessive.
5. Reassemble the components, ensuring that the chamfered end of the outer rotor is innermost in the pump body.

Data
Rotor end-float .. .. 0·127 mm (0·005 in)
Diametral clearance of outer rotor to pump body 0·254 mm (0·010 in)
Rotor lobe clearance .. .. 0·152 mm (0·006 in) maximum

 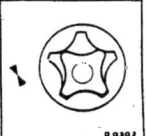

Section C7

CAMSHAFT BEARING LINERS

1. Withdraw the front bearing liner, using the tools shown in Fig. 1.

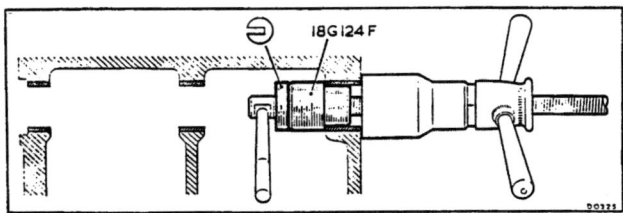

Fig. 1

2. Withdraw the rear bearing liner, using the tools shown in Fig. 2.

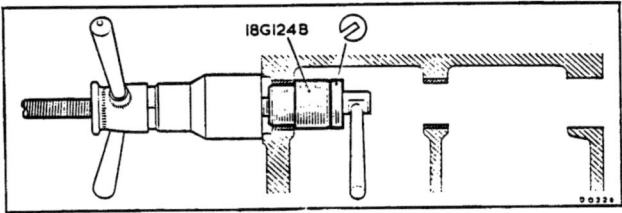

Fig. 2

50D
DIESEL ENGINE

3. Withdraw the centre bearing liner, using the tools shown in Fig. 3.

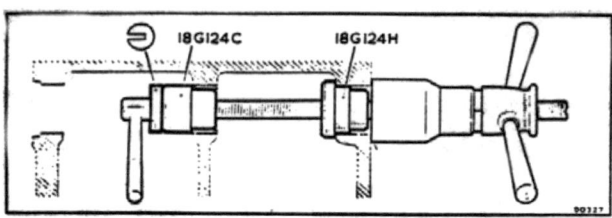

Fig. 3

4. Fit a new front bearing liner, using the tools shown in Fig. 4, and lining up the oil holes in the liner with those in the crankcase.

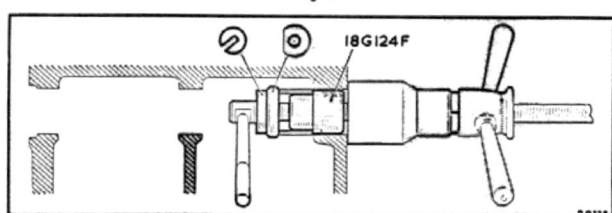

Fig. 4

5. Fit a new rear bearing liner, lining up the oil holes and using the tools shown in Fig. 5.

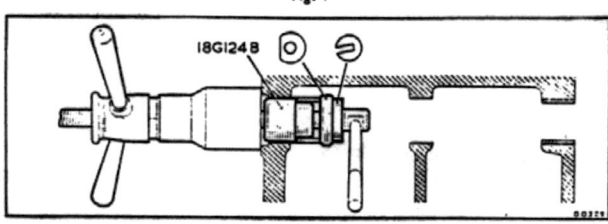

Fig. 5

6. Fit a new centre bearing liner, lining up the oil holes and using the tools shown in Fig. 6.

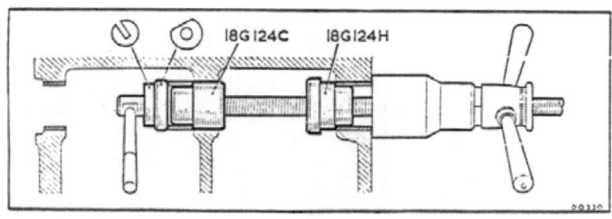

Fig. 6

7. Ream the front and rear bearing liners, using the tools shown in Fig. 7.

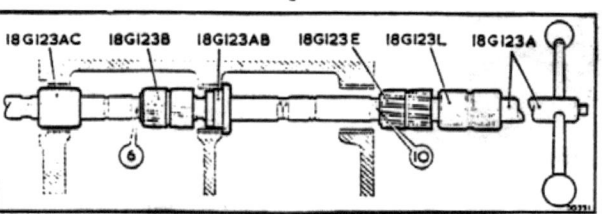

Fig. 7

DIESEL ENGINE 50D

8. Ream the centre bearing liner, using the tools shown in Fig. 8.

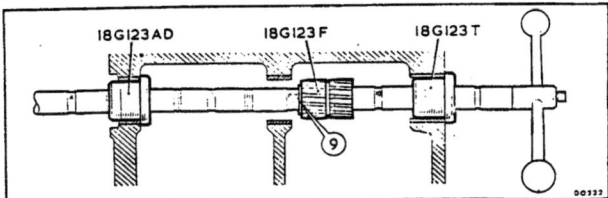

Fig. 8

Section C8

FLYWHEEL

1. If the teeth on the starter ring are worn or damaged, remove the starter ring by drilling a hole and splitting the ring across the hole with a hammer and chisel.
2. Heat the new starter ring uniformly to a temperature between 200 and 230°C (392 and 446°F); the strip of temperature-indicating paint on the ring will change from pink to grey at the correct temperature.
3. Fit the starter ring with the tooth chamfer facing away from the flywheel register.

Section C9

CYLINDER BORES

1. If the cylinder bores cannot be cleaned up at the maximum oversize given in Data, bore them to the dimension given for fitting cylinder liners.
2. Press in the cylinder liners and then bore them to the standard bore size.

Data

Cylinder bore:
  Standard .. ..   73·01 to 73·02 mm (2·8745 to 2·876 in)
  Oversizes: First .. ..   0·254 mm (0·010 in)
          Second (maximum if linered)   0·508 mm (0·020 in)
          Third .. ..   0·762 mm (0·030 in)
          Fourth (maximum) .. ..   1·02 mm (0·040 in)
  Bore size for fitting liners .. ..   76·62 to 76·63 mm (3·0165 to 3·017 in)

51D

FUEL SYSTEM

Section C8

MAIN FILTER

1. Unscrew the centre bolt and remove the filter base and element.
2. Check the operation of the non-return valve in No. 4 connection.
3. Renew the filter element, and the 'O' ring and sealing rings in the filter head and base.
4. Reassemble the filter components as shown in Fig. 1.

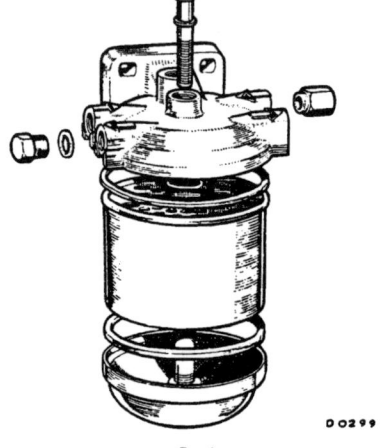

Fig. 1

DIESEL ENGINE

Section C10

CONNECTING ROD AND PISTON

1. Separate the piston from the connecting rod.
2. Check the gudgeon pin clearance in the little-end bush against the figure in Data. If the clearance is excessive, renew the little-end bush.
   a. Position the new bush with its joint on the cap side of the connecting rod as shown in Fig. 1.
   b. Finish-ream the bush to the size given in Data.
3. Check the piston ring groove clearance and the piston ring gap against the figures in Data. Renew the rings, or piston and rings, as necessary.
4. Assemble the piston to the connecting rod with the combustion cavity and oil jet hole in line as shown in Fig. 2.

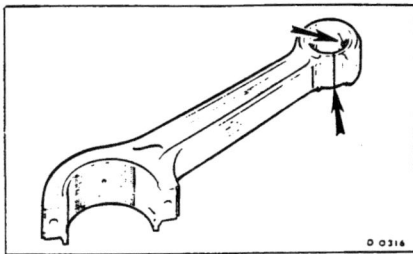

Fig. 1

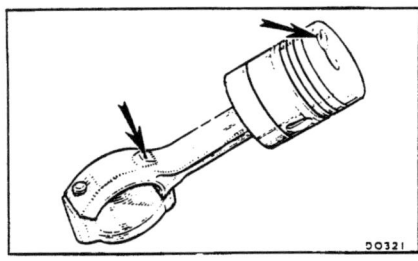

Fig. 2

Data

Little-end bush finish reamed diameter	25·399 to 25·452 mm (0·9999 to 1·00025 in)
Diameter	25·394 to 25·4 mm (0·9998 to 1·0 in)
Fit in piston	0·009 mm (0·00035 in) clearance to 0·001 mm (0·00005 in) interference
Fit in connecting rod	0·005 to 0·023 mm (0·0002 to 0·0009 in) clearance
Piston to bore clearance at bottom of skirt	0·091 to 0·106 mm (0·0036 to 0·0042 in)
Ring/groove clearance:	
Top compression	0·09 to 0·14 mm (0·0035 to 0·0055 in)
2nd and 3rd compression	0·063 to 0·114 mm (0·0025 to 0·0045 in)
Oil control	0·051 to 0·102 mm (0·002 to 0·004 in)
Ring gap:	
Top, compression	0·305 to 0·432 mm (0·012 to 0·017 in)
Remainder	0·203 to 0·330 mm (0·008 to 0·013 in)

51D

FUEL SYSTEM

Section B1

LIFT PUMP

Removing
1. Disconnect both fuel pipes from the lift pump.
2. Remove the nuts securing the lift pump to the engine and detach the pump.

Refitting
3. Reverse the procedure in 1 and 2, noting:
   a. Renew the gasket between the pump and engine if necessary.
   b. Bleed the fuel system (see 'MAINTENANCE').

Section B2

MAIN FUEL FILTER

Removing
1. Disconnect the fuel pipes from the filter head.
2. Remove the bolts securing the filter to its bracket and detach the filter assembly.

Refitting
3. Reverse the procedure in 1 and 2, and bleed the fuel system (see 'MAINTENANCE').

Section B3

FUEL INJECTION PUMP

Removing
1. Detach the fuel feed and return pipes from the injection pump and the fuel filter.
2. Detach the high pressure pipes from the pump and the injectors.
3. Disconnect the stop and throttle control cables at their trunnions on the pump levers.
4. Remove the nuts retaining the cable stop bracket to the pump and detach the bracket complete with cables.
5. Remove the nuts and washers retaining the pump to the engine and withdraw the pump from the engine.

Refitting
6. Reverse the procedure in 1 to 5, noting:
   a. Position the crankshaft and set the injection timing pointer as described in 'MAINTENANCE'.
   b. Fit the injection pump so that the mark on its mounting flange lines up with the timing pointer.
   c. Bleed the fuel system (see 'MAINTENANCE').
   d. Adjust the maximum and idling speeds to the figures given in 'GENERAL DATA'.

FUEL SYSTEM 51D

Section B4

INJECTORS

Removing
1. Disconnect the spill pipes and the high-pressure pipes from the injectors.
2. Remove the injector securing nuts and withdraw the injectors using tool 18G 491 A.

Refitting
3. Renew the atomizer sealing washers, fitting new washers as shown in Fig. 1.
4. Reverse the procedure in 1 and 2, and bleed the high pressure pipes.

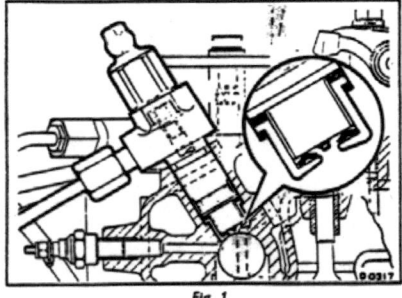

Fig. 1

MAINTENANCE

BLEEDING THE FUEL SYSTEM

1. Ensure that there is an adequate supply of fuel in the tank.
2. Slacken the union at the filter end of the injection pump feed pipe. Operate the lift pump by hand, and when the fuel coming from the slackened union is free of air bubbles, tighten the union.
3. Slacken the plug in the unused connection in the filter head. Operate the lift pump, and when fuel coming from the connection is free of air bubbles, tighten the plug.
4. Slacken the two bleed valves on the injection pump illustrated in Fig. 1. Operate the lift pump, and when fuel coming from both valves is free of air bubbles, tighten the valves.
5. Slacken the unions at the injector ends of any two high-pressure pipes. Ensure that the stop control is in the run position and the throttle in the fully open position. Crank the engine until the fuel coming from both pipes is free of air bubbles, then tighten the unions.
6. Start the engine and allow it to run until it is running on all four cylinders.

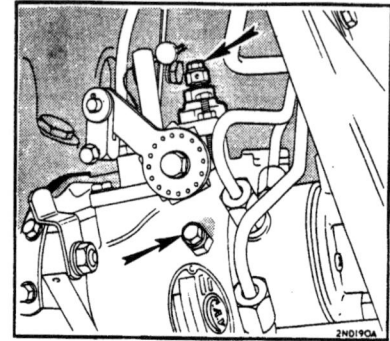

Fig. 1

WARNING: As the injection pump is lubricated by fuel under pressure, no attempt should be made to bleed the system by towing a vehicle in gear.

INJECTION TIMING ADJUSTMENT

1. Set No. 1 piston at 22° B.T.D.C. on compression stroke.
2. Set the scriber arm MS67A/2B to 208° on the universal timing gauge MS67A and lock in position.
3. Engage the timing gauge splined shaft with the injection pump drive and slide the gauge body up to the mounting face. Lock the body to the shaft with the nylon screw.
4. Eliminate backlash by light clockwise pressure on the gauge.
5. Set the pointer, if necessary, to align with the scribing edge.
6. Remove the timing gauge.
7. Position the injection pump so that the mark on its mounting flange is aligned with the timing pointer.

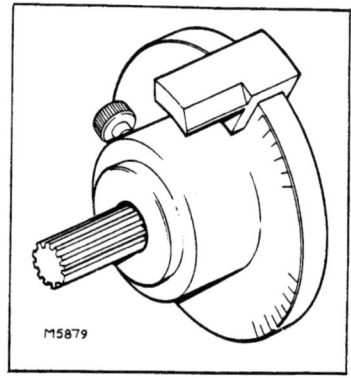

MAINTENANCE

VALVE ROCKER CLEARANCE ADJUSTMENT

The correct clearance between the valve rockers and the valve stem is given in 'GENERAL DATA'. Remove the rocker cover and check the clearance between the rocker and the valve stem in the order shown below.

Adjust No. 1 rocker with No. 8 valve fully open
,, ,, 3 ,, ,, ,, 6 ,, ,, ,,
,, ,, 5 ,, ,, ,, 4 ,, ,, ,,
,, ,, 2 ,, ,, ,, 7 ,, ,, ,,
,, ,, 8 ,, ,, ,, 1 ,, ,, ,,
,, ,, 6 ,, ,, ,, 3 ,, ,, ,,
,, ,, 4 ,, ,, ,, 5 ,, ,, ,,
,, ,, 7 ,, ,, ,, 2 ,, ,, ,,

Adjust if necessary, by slackening the locking nut and turning the adjusting screw in the appropriate direction until the clearance is correct. Hold the screw against rotation and tighten the locking nut. Refit the rocker cover and check that its gasket is serviceable.

GOVERNED SPEED ADJUSTMENT

With the engine at normal running temperature make the following settings:

1. Set the maximum speed stop screw to give 4400 rev/min.
2. Set the idling stop screw to give 500 to 600 rev/min.
3. Open the throttle a little to give a slight increase in rev/min.
4. Unscrew the idling damper adjusting screw one-third of a turn.
5. Run the engine at three-quarter of maximum rev/min. and release the throttle.
   a. If the engine stalls, screw the damper adjusting screw in slightly.
   b. If engine die-down is sluggish, screw the damper adjusting screw out slightly.
6. Check the operation of the stop control.

BMC (LEYLAND)

1,8 LITRE DIESEL ENGINE

REPAIR
OPERATION MANUAL

SPECIFICATION

Purchasers are advised that the specification details set out in this Manual apply to a range of engines and not to any particular engine. For the specification of any particular engine purchasers should consult their supplier.

The manufacturers reserve the right to vary their specifications with or without notice, and at such times and in such manner as they think fit. Major as well as minor changes may be involved in accordance with the manufacturer's policy of constant product improvement. ment.

Whilst every effort is made to ensure the accuracy of the particulars contained in this Manual, neither the manufacturer nor the supplier, by whom this Manual is supplied, shall in any circumstances be held liable for any inaccuracy or the consequences thereof.

CONTENTS

	Operation No.	Page No.
General Specification Data	04	7
Engine Tuning Data	05	9
Torque Wrench Settings	06	9
Service Lubricants, Fuel, Fluids and Capacities	09	10

MAINTENANCE 10

Routine Maintenance Operations
- Engine 10–1
- Fuel System 10–2
- Electrical 10–2
- Service Operations 10–2

ENGINE

Camshaft
- bearings – remove and refit . . . . 12.13.13 . . . 12–2
- locating plate – remove and refit (see 12.65.12) . . . . 12.13.23 . . . 12–13
- remove and refit (see 12.29.57) . . . . 12.13.02 . . . 12–1

Connecting rods and pistons
- overhaul . . . . 12.17.10 . . . 12–5
- remove and refit . . . . 12.17.01 . . . 12–4

Crankshaft
- end-float – check and adjust . . . . 12.21.26 . . . 12–6
- front oil seal – remove and refit (see 12.65.05) . . . . 12.21.14 . . . 12–13
- rear oil seal – remove and refit . . . . 12.21.20 . . . 12–5
- remove and refit . . . . 12.21.33 . . . 12–6
- spigot bush – remove and refit . . . . 12.21.45 . . . 12–7

Cylinder head
- gasket – remove and refit . . . . 12.29.02 . . . 12–9
- overhaul . . . . 12.29.19 . . . 12–10
- rocker shaft – overhaul . . . . 12.29.55 . . . 12–11
- rocker shaft – remove and refit . . . . 12.29.54 . . . 12–11
- tappets – remove and refit . . . . 12.29.57 . . . 12–1
- valve clearance – check and adjust . . . . 12.29.48 . . . 12–11

Cylinder liners – remove and refit . . . . 12.25.26 . . . 12–8

Engine
- front mounting plate gasket – remove and refit . . . . . . 12.25.10 . . . 12–8
- governed speeds – check and adjust . . . . 12.49.12 . . . 12–12

Flywheel
- gearbox adaptor plate – remove and refit (see 12.21.20) 12.53.03 . . . 12–5
- remove and refit (see 12.21.20) . . . . 12.53.07 . . . 12–5

Lubrication
- oil pick-up strainer – remove and refit (see 12.10.30) . . . 12.60.20 . . . 12–1
- oil pressure relief valve – remove and refit . . . . 12.60.56 . . . 12–13
- oil pump drive shaft – remove and refit . . . . 12.10.30 . . . 12–1
- oil pump – overhaul . . . . 12.60.32 . . . 12–12
- oil pump – remove and refit (see 12.10.30) . . . . 12.60.26 . . . 12–1

Timing gears, chains and tensioners
- cover oil seal – remove and refit . . . . 12.65.05 . . . 12–13
- cover – remove and refit (see 12.65.05) . . . . 12.65.01 . . . 12–13
- fuel injection pump gear – remove and refit . . . . 12.10.25 . . . 12–1
- fuel injection pump hub – remove and refit . . . . 12.10.26 . . . 12–1
- tensioner – remove and refit (see 12.65.12) . . . . 12.65.28 . . . 12–13
- timing chain and gears – remove and refit . . . . 12.65.12 . . . 12–13
- timing chain – remove and refit . . . . 12.65.14 . . . 12–13

continued

CONTENTS

	Operation No.	
FUEL SYSTEM		
Fuel filter element — remove and refit	19.25.07	19–3
Fuel system — bleeding	19.50.07	19–11
Injection pump		
— overhaul	19.30.19	19–6
— remove and refit . . .	19.30.07	19–5
— timing — check and adjust	19.30.01	19–5
Injectors		
— overhaul	19.60.08	19–12
— remove and refit . . .	19.60.01	19–12
Lift pump		
— overhaul	19.45.16	19–11
— remove and refit	19.45.09	19–11
COOLING SYSTEM		
Coolant — drain and refill	26.10.01	
Fan		
— belt — remove and refit	26.20.07	26–1
— blades — remove and refit	26.25.01	26–1
— pulley — remove and refit	26.25.01	26–1
Thermostat		
— remove and refit	26.45.01	26–
— test	26.45.09	26–
Water pump — remove and refit	26.50.01	
CLUTCH		
Clutch assembly		
— overhaul	33.10.08	33–1
— remove and refit	33.10.01	33–1
Clutch driven plate — remove and refit (see 33.10.01) .	33.10.02	33–
Release bearing — remove and refit	33.25.12	33–2
ELECTRICAL		
Alternator		
— overhaul	86.10.08	86–2
— remove and refit	86.10.02	86–2
Service precautions	86.01.01	86–1
Starter motor		
— overhaul	86.60.13	86–3
— remove and refit	86.60.01	86–3
Starter solenoid		
— remove and refit	86.60.08	86–3
Testing the charging circuit	86.01.02	

SERVICE TOOLS   End of manual

INTRODUCTION

The purpose of this Manual is to assist skilled mechanics in the efficient repair and maintenance of the range of engines given on the title-page. The procedures detailed, carried out in the sequence given and using the appropriate service tools, will enable the operations to be completed in the time stated in the Repair Operation Times.

Indexing

The contents pages list the titles and reference numbers of the divisions in alphabetical order.

Operation Numbering

Each operation is followed by the number allocated to it in a master index. The number consists of six digits arranged in three pairs.

The master index of operations has been compiled for universal application to engines manufactured by BL Cars Limited and therefore continuity of the numbering sequence is not maintained throughout this Manual.

Each instruction within an operation has a sequence number, and to complete the operation in the minimum time it is essential that these instructions are performed in the numerical sequence commencing at 1 unless otherwise stated. Where applicable, the sequence numbers identify the components in the appropriate illustration.

Service Tools

Where performance of an operation requires the use of a service tool, the tool number is quoted under the operation heading and is repeated in the instruction involving its use.

An illustrated list of all service tools necessary to complete the operations described in the Manual is also included.

Definitions

Remove and refit — the removing of an existing part, fitting of a new or replacement part.
Overhaul — includes removing a component, fitting new parts, adjusting and its refitting.

References

The water pump end of the engine is referred to as the front.

To reduce repetition, operations covered in this Manual do not include reference to testing the engine after repair. It is essential that work is inspected and tested after completion, particularly where safety-related items are concerned.

Dimensions

The dimensions quoted are to design engineering specification. Alternative unit equivalents have been converted from the original specification.

During the period of running-in from new, certain adjustments may vary from the specification figures given in this Manual. These adjustments will be reset by the supplier at the After Sales Service, and thereafter should be maintained at the figures specified in the Manual.

REPAIRS AND REPLACEMENTS

When service parts are required it is essential that only genuine BL or Unipart replacements are used.

Attention is particularly drawn to the following points concerning repairs and the fitting of replacements parts and accessories:

The performance and durability of the engine may be impaired if other than genuine parts are fitted. In certain territories, legislation prohibits the fitting of parts not to the engine manufacturer's specification. Torque wrench setting figures given in this Manual must be strictly adhered to. Locking devices, where specified, must be fitted. If the efficiency of a locking device is impaired during removal, it must be renewed. When purchasing accessories while travelling abroad ensure that the accessory and its fitted location conform to the requirements existing in their country of origin. The engine warranty may be invalidated by the fitting of other than genuine BL or Unipart parts.

All BL and Unipart replacements have the full backing of the factory warranty.

SERVICE PARTS

Genuine BL and UNIPART Service parts are designed and tested for your engine and have the full backing of the BL Factory Warranty. ONLY WHEN GENUINE BL OR UNIPART SERVICE PARTS ARE USED CAN RESPONSIBILITY BE CONSIDERED UNDER THE TERMS OF THE WARRANTY.

Genuine parts are supplied in cartons bearing one or both of these symbols:

ABBREVIATIONS AND SYMBOLS IN THIS MANUAL

Across flats (bolt size)	A.F.	Gallons (Imperial)	gal	Miles per gallon	m.p.g.	Revolutions per minute	rev/min
After bottom dead centre	A.B.D.C.	Gallons (U.S.)	U.S. gal	Miles per hour	m.p.h.	Right-hand	R.H.
After top dead centre	A.T.D.C.	Grammes (force)	gf	Millimetres	mm	Right-hand steering	R.H.Stg.
Alternating current	a.c.	Grammes (mass)	g	Millimetres of mercury	mmHg		"
Amperes	A			Minimum	min.	Second (angle)	2nd
Ampere-hour	Ah	High compression	h.c	Minus (of tolerance)	−	Second (numerical order)	SC
Atmospheres	Atm	High tension (electrical)	h.t.	Minute (of angle)	'	Single carburetter	
		Horse-power	hp			Society of Automobile Engineers	S.A.E.
Before bottom dead centre	B.B.D.C.	Hundredweight	cv	Negative (electrical)	−	Specific gravity	sp. gr.
Before top dead centre	B.T.D.C.			Newton metre	Nm	Square centimetres	cm²
Bottom dead centre	B.D.C.	Inches	in	Number	No.	Square inches	in²
Brake horse power	b.h.p.	Inches of mercury	inHg			Standard	std.
Brake mean effective pressure	b.m.e.p.	Independent front suspension	i.f.s.	Ounces (force)	ozf	Standard wire gauge	s.w.g.
British Standards	B.S.	Internal diameter	i.dia.	Ounces (mass)	oz	Synchronizer/synchromesh	synchro.
				Ounce inch (torque)	ozf in		
Carbon monoxide	CO	Kilogrammes (force)	kgf	Outside diameter	o.dia	Third	3rd
Centigrade (Celsius)	C	Kilogrammes (mass)	kg	Overdrive	O/D	Top dead centre	T.D.C.
Centimetres	cm	Kilogramme centimetre	kgf cm			Twin carburetters	TC
Cubic centimetres	cm³	Kilogramme metres	kgf m	Paragraphs	para.		
Cubic inches	in³	Kilogrammes per square centimetre	kgf/cm²	Part Number	Part No.	United Kingdom	UK
Cycles per minute	c/min	Kilometres	km	Percentage	%		
		Kilometres per hour	km/h	Pints (Imperial)	pt	Volts	V
Degree (angle)	deg. or °	Kilovolts	kV	Pints (U.S.)	U.S. pt		
Degree (temperature)	deg. or °	King pin inclination	k.p.i.	Plus or minus	±	Watts	W
Diameter	dia.			Plus (tolerance)	+		
Direct current	d.c.	Left-hand	L.H.	Positive (electrical)	+	Screw threads	
		Left-hand steering	L.H.Stg.	Pounds (force)	lbf	American Standard Taper Pipe	N.P.T.F.
Fahrenheit	F	Left-hand thread	L.H.Thd.	Pounds (mass)	lb	British Association	B.A.
Feet	ft	Low compression	l.c.	Pounds feet (torque)	lbf ft	British Standard Fine	B.S.F.
Feet per minute	ft/min	Low tension	l.t.	Pounds inches (torque)	lbf in	British Standard Pipe	B.S.P.
Fifth	5th			Pounds per square inch	lbf/in²	British Standard Whitw	B.S.W
Figure (illustration)	Fig.	Maximum	max.			Unified Coarse	U.N.C
First	1st	Metres	m	Radius	r	Unified Fine	U.N.F
Fourth	4th	Miniature Edison Screw	MES	Ratio			
				Reference	ref.		

GENERAL SPECIFICATION DATA

The symbol ① in this Manual refers to engines with engine numbers prior to:

18P/885B/D1102   18V/738B/D460   18V/745B/D251
                  18V/744B/D1900I 18V/886B/D501

The symbol ② refers to engines with engine numbers commencing at those above, and all engine numbers beginning 18B/919B/D or 18V/920B/D or 18P/830A/D. ℮ 18V/258 D

ENGINE — Diesel 1.8 litre

Type	18V — — — D
Number of cylinders	4
Bore	3.16 in (80.26 mm)
Stroke	3.5 in (88.9 mm)
Capacity	109.8 in³ (1799 cm³)
Injection order	1, 3, 4, 2
Valve operation	Overhead by push-rod
Compression ratio: ① **	21.47 : 1
②	22.3 : 1
Torque (gross) ②	107 Nm, 79 lbf ft, 10.92 kgf m at 2,400 rev/min

Crankshaft

Main journal diameter	2.1262 to 2.1270 in (54.01 to 54.03 mm)
Crankpin journal diameter	1.8759 to 1.8764 in (47.64 to 47.65 mm)
Crankshaft end-thrust	Taken on thrust washers at centre main bearing
Crankshaft end-float	0.001 to 0.0055 in (0.025 to 0.139 mm)

Main bearings

Number and type	5 Steel backed lead indium
Length: Front, centre and rear	1.120 to 1.130 in (28.45 to 28.70 mm)
Intermediate	0.760 to 0.770 in (19.30 to 19.55 mm)
Diametrical clearance	0.001 to 0.0027 in (0.03 to 0.07 mm)

Connecting rods

Type	Horizontally split big-end, plain small end
Length between centres	6.220 to 6.222 in (157.9 to 158.0 mm)

Big-end bearings

Type	Steel backed lead indium
Length	0.775 to 0.785 in (19.68 to 19.93 mm)
Diametrical clearance	0.001 to 0.0027 in (0.03 to 0.07 mm)

Gudgeon pin

Type	Fully floating with circlip location
Fit in piston	0.0001 to 0.0003 in (0.002 to 0.007 mm) clearance
Fit in connecting rod	0.0002 to 0.0009 in (0.02 to 0.04 mm) clearance
Diameter (outer)	0.9998 to 1.0000 in (25.39 to 25.40 mm)

Pistons

Type	Aluminium alloy, solid skirt, with open combustion cavity
Clearances:	
Top land	0.0171 to 0.0211 in (0.43 to 0.57 mm)
Bottom land	0.0137 to 0.0172 in (0.35 to 0.44 mm)
Bottom of skirt	0.004 to 0.005 in (0.10 to 0.13 mm)
Oversizes	0.020 in (0.51 mm)

Piston rings

Compression:	
Type: Top	Chrome-faced
Second	Tapered, cast iron alloy
Width	0.0771 to 0.0781 in (1.96 to 1.98 mm)
Fitted gap: Top	0.012 to 0.017 in (0.30 to 0.43 mm)
Second	0.009 to 0.014 in (0.23 to 0.35 mm)
Ring to groove clearance: Top	0.0025 to 0.0045 in (0.06 to 0.11 mm)
Second	0.0015 to 0.0035 in (0.04 to 0.09 mm)
Oil control	
Type	Slotted scraper
Fitted gap	0.012 to 0.017 in (0.30 to 0.43 mm)
Ring to groove clearance	0.0015 to 0.0035 in (0.04 to 0.09 mm)

Camshaft ①

Journal diameters: Front	1.78875 to 1.78925 in (45.43 to 45.44 mm)
Centre	1.72875 to 1.72925 in (43.91 to 43.93 mm)
Rear	1.62275 to 1.62325 in (41.22 to 41.23 mm)
Bearing liner inside diameter (reamed after fitting):	
Front	1.79025 to 1.79075 in (45.47 to 45.48 mm)
Centre	1.73025 to 1.73075 in (43.95 to 43.96 mm)
Rear	1.62425 to 1.62475 in (40.26 to 40.27 mm)
Diametrical clearance	0.001 to 0.002 in (0.02 to 0.05 mm)
End-thrust	Taken on locating plate
End-float	0.003 to 0.007 in (0.08 to 0.18 mm)

Camshaft ②

Journal diameters: Front	1.95125 to 1.95175 in (49.652 to 49.574 mm)
Centre	1.91975 to 1.92025 in (48.762 to 48.774 mm)
Rear	1.72875 to 1.72925 in (43.910 to 43.923 mm)
Diametral clearance	0.001 to 0.002 in (0.02 to 0.05 mm)
End-thrust	Taken on locating plate
End-float	0.003 to 0.007 in (0.08 to 0.18 mm)

Rocker gear

Rocker shaft diameter	0.624 to 0.625 in (15.85 to 15.87 mm)
Rocker bush inside diameter (reamed in position)	0.6255 to 0.6260 in (15.89 to 15.90 mm)

Tappets

Type	Bucket
Outside diameter	0.8125 in (20.65 mm)
Length	1.495 to 1.505 in (37.97 to 38.23 mm)

** ① ② see page 7

continued

Valves

Seat angle: Inlet	45°
Exhaust	45°
Head diameter: Inlet	1.434 to 1.439 in (36.42 to 36.55 mm)
Exhaust	1.207 to 1.212 in (30.64 to 30.78 mm)
Stem diameter: Inlet	0.3428 to 0.3433 in (8.71 to 8.73 mm)
Exhaust	0.3422 to 0.3427 in (8.69 to 8.70 mm)
Stem to guide clearance: Inlet	0.0008 to 0.0020 in (0.02 to 0.05 mm)
Exhaust	0.0014 to 0.0026 in (0.03 to 0.06 mm)
Valve lift: Inlet and exhaust	0.384 in (9.75 mm)
Valve stand down: [1] **	0.0445 to 0.0505 in (1.13 to 1.28 mm)
[2]	0.020 to 0.030 in (0.508 to 0.762 mm)

Valve guides

Length: Inlet and exhaust	2.22 in (56.39 mm)
Outside diameter: Inlet and exhaust	0.5635 to 0.5640 in (14.31 to 14.33 mm)
Inside diameter (reamed after fitting): Inlet and exhaust	0.3441 to 0.3448 in (8.74 to 8.76 mm)
Fitted height above spring seat: Inlet and exhaust	0.55 to 0.56 in (13.9 to 14.2 mm)
Interference fit in head: Inlet and exhaust	0.0005 to 0.00175 in (0.01 to 0.04 mm)

Valve springs

Free length	1.92 in (48.77 mm)
Fitted length	1.44 in (36.57 mm)
Load at fitted length	82 lbf, 37.19 kgf, 364 N
Load at top of lift	142 lbf, 64.4 kgf, 631 N
Number of working coils	4½

Valve timing

Timing marks	Dimples on timing wheels, marks on flywheel
Rocker clearance: [1] **Running	0.017 in (0.43 mm)
Timing	0.024 in (0.61 mm)
[2] Running	0.014 in (0.36 mm)
Timing	0.016 in (0.41 mm)

	[1]		[2]	
Inlet valve: Opens	8° B.T.D.C.		8° B.T.D.C.	
Closes	42° A.B.D.C.		44° A.B.D.C.	
Exhaust valve: Opens	60° B.B.D.C.		50° B.B.D.C.	
Closes	12° A.T.D.C.		10° A.T.D.C.	

Lubrication

System	Wet sump, pressure fed
System pressure: Running	3.5 bar, 50 lbf/in², 3.52 kgf/cm²
Idling	1.0 bar, 15 lbf/in², 1.05 kgf/cm²
Oil pump	Rotor type
Oil filter	Full flow; disposable cartridge type
Oil pressure relief valve	3.5 bar, 50 lbf/in², 3.52 kgf/cm²
Relief valve springs: Free length	3 in (76 mm)
Fitted length	2.156 in (54.77 mm)
Load at fitted length	15.5 to 16.5 lbf, 7.0 to 7.4 kgf, 69 to 73 N

FUEL SYSTEM

Fuel injection pump	C.A.V
Type	DPA.3247F180, DPA.3247F260, DPA.3342F710 or DPA3342F720
Injection timing	18° B.T.D.C.
Fuel lift pump	A.C. Mechanical
Fuel injectors	C.A.V. Pintaux
Nozzle type	BDN.OSPC.6651
Nozzle holder type	BKB.35SD.5188
Opening pressure	135 Atm
Main fuel filter	C.A.V.
Type	FS583 6B130
Heater plugs	
Champion	AG32

COOLING SYSTEM

Thermostat:	
Standard	82° C (180° F)
Hot climates	72° C (162° F)
Cold climates	88° C (190° F)
Fan belt tension	See 'Maintenance'

CLUTCH

Type	Single dry plate
Clutch plate diameter	9 in (228.6 mm)

ELECTRICAL

Alternator

	16ACR	18ACR
Type: Lucas	34 A	43 A
Output at 14V and 6000 rev/min		
Rotor winding resistance at 20°C (68°F)	3.3 ohm ± 5%	3.2 ohm ± 5%
Maximum permissible rotor speed	15 000 rev/min	15 000 rev/min
Brush length new	0.5 in (12.7 mm)	0.5 in (12.7 mm)
Brush spring tension, brush face flush with brush box	3 to 4 N, 9 to 13 ozf, 255 to 368 gf	3 to 4 N, 9 to 13 ozf, 255 to 368 gf

Starter motor

Type: Lucas	M45G pre-engaged
Light running current	100 amp at 5000 to 6000 rev/min
Lock torque at 940 amp	29 lbf ft (4.01 kgf m, 39 Nm)
Minimum brush length	0.31 in (8.0 mm)
Brush spring tension	4 2 ozf (1.2 kgf, 11 N)

** [1] [2] see page 7

ENGINE TUNING DATA

ENGINE — Diesel 1.8 litre

Type	18—/——/D
Displacement	109.7 in³ (1798 cm³)
Injection order	1, 3, 4, 2
Compression ratio	21.47 : 1
Valve rocker clearance (cold) [1]**	0.017 in (0.43 mm)
[2]	0.014 in (0.36 mm)
Idle speed:	
Engines with hydraulic governer	650 rev/min minimum †
Engines with mechanical governer	800 rev/min minimum †
Maximum governed light running speed	4,900 rev/min †
Fuel injection pump	
Make and type	C.A.V. DPA.3247F180, DPA.3247F260, DPA.3342F710 or DPA.3342F720
Injection pump timing	18° B.T.D.C.
Fuel injectors	
Make and type	C.A.V. Pintaux
Nozzle type	BDN.OSPC.6651
Nozzle holder type	BKB.35SD.5188
Opening pressure	135 Atm
Heater plugs	
Make and type	Champion AG32

For exact settings see injection pump code and/or Equipment manufacturers settings.

** [1] [2] see page 7

TORQUE WRENCH SETTINGS

	lbf ft	kgf m	Nm
Cylinder head nuts	75	10.4	102
Rocker bracket nuts	25	3.5	34
Manifold nuts	15	2.1	20
Big-end nuts	35	4.8	47
Main bearing set screws	75	10.4	102
Flywheel bolts	40	5.5	54
Timing cover bolts: ¼ in	6	0.8	8
⅜ in	20	2.8	27
Rear plate bolts: ¼ in	20	2.8	27
⅜ in	30	4.1	41
Camshaft nut	65	9.0	88
Crankshaft bolt	115*	16	156
Idler gear hub bolt	30	4.1	41
Cylinder side cover set screws	4	0.5	5
Rocker cover nuts	4	0.5	5
Sump bolts	6	0.8	8
Oil filter adaptor	30	4.1	41
Oil pump nuts	16	2.2	22
Oil release valve — domed nut	45	6.2	61
Starter motor bolts	35	4.8	47
Clutch to flywheel	25	3.5	34
Fuel lift pump nuts	12	1.7	16
Injector nozzle nut	50	6.9	68
Injection pump nuts	18	2.5	24
Injector nuts	12	1.7	16
Injection pump driving flange set screws	10	1.4	14
Water pump nuts	17	2.3	23
Water pump bolts	18	2.5	24
Alternator pulley nut	27	3.7	36
Thermal transmitter	16	2.2	22

*Discard lock washer

SERVICE LUBRICANTS, FUEL, FLUIDS AND CAPACITIES

Lubricants

The lubrication system of your new engine is filled with high quality oil. You should always use a high quality oil of the correct viscosity range in the engine during subsequent maintenance operations or when topping up. The use of oils not to the correct specification can lead to high oil and fuel consumption and ultimately to damage to components.

Oil to the correct specification contains additives which dispense the corrosive acids formed by combustion and also prevent the formation of sludge which can block oilways. Additional oil additives should not be used. Service intervals must be adhered to.

Engine

Use a well known brand of oil to B.L.S. OL02 or MIL-L-2104B or MIL-L-46152 or A.P.I. SE/CC quality, with a viscosity band spanning the temperature range of your locality.

The use of monograde oils is permissible providing that it is of the correct viscosity for the ambient temperature of your locality. It should also be of the same quality MIL-L-46152, MIL-L-2104B or A.P.I. SE/CC as the preferred multigrade oils.

For sustained high speed operation or operation for long periods in a high ambient temperature, the use of a multigrade oil of the correct viscosity and quality is recommended.

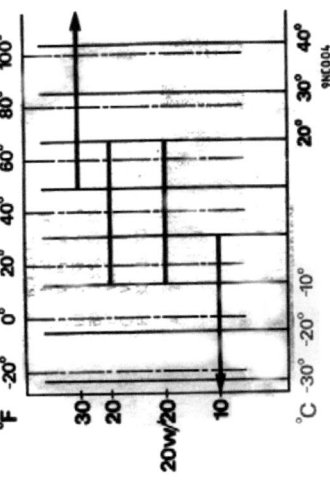

S.A.E. Viscosity

Monograde Oils Viscosity/Temperature Ranges

Multigrade Oils Viscosity/Temperature Ranges

S.A.E. Viscosity

Fuel

Use fuel oils generally known as Diesel fuel oil, distillate Diesel fuel, automotive gas oil or Derv fuel conforming to British Standard 2869: 1967, Class A1 or A2.

Anti-Freeze Solutions

Use UNIPART UNIVERSAL Anti-freeze to protect the cooling system.

If UNIPART Universal is not available any anti-freeze conforming to Specification B.S. 3151 or 3152 may be used. Anti-freezes to these specifications are compatible with UNIPART Universal and can be used with it. UNIPART Universal should not be mixed with other universal anti-freezes.

The overall anti-freeze concentration should not fall below 30% by volume, to ensure that the anti-corrosion properties of the coolant are maintained.

After filling with anti-freeze solution, attach a warning label in a prominent position stating the type of anti-freeze contained in the cooling system to ensure that the correct type is used for topping-up.

Solution	Commences to freeze		Frozen solid	
%	°C	°F	°C	°F
33⅓	−19	−2	−36	−33
50	−36	−33	−48	−53

Capacities (approx.)
Engine sump (including filter) . . . . 8¾ pt, 4.68 litres, 9.9 U.S. pt
Filter only . . . . 1¼ pt, 0.71 litre, 1.5 U.S. pt

LUBRICANTS

		FORECOURT OILS			FLEET OIL	
Minimum performance level		MIL-L-2104B A.P.I.-SE/CC or MIL-L-46152				
Climatic Conditions	Temperatures above −10°C (10°F)	Temperatures −20°C (−5°F) to 10°C (50°F)	Temperatures below −10°C (10°F)	Temperatures above −10°C (10°F)	Temperatures −20°C (−5°F) to 10°C (50°F)	Temperatures below −10°C (10°F)
UNIPART	Unipart Super Multigrade Motor Oil 15W/50					
BP	BP Super Visco-Static 20W/50 BP Vanellus C3 Multi-grade BP Visco 2000*	BP Super Visco Static 10W/30 or 10W/40*	BP Super Visco-Static 5W/20*	BP Vanellus M 20–50 BP Vanellus C3 Multigrade	BP Vanellus M 10W/30 or 10W/40*	BP Super Visco-Static 5W/20*
CASTROL	Castrol GTX 20W/50 Castrol GTX-2 15W/20	Castrolite 10W/30 or 10W/40 Castrol GTZ 10W/40 (Sweden)	Castrol Super GTX 5W/30 (Canada) Castrol GTZ 5W/40 (Finland)	Castrol Deusol RX Super 15W/40		
DUCKHAMS	Duckhams Q Motor Oil 20W/50		*Not available in the U.K.	Fleetol Multi-V 20W/50 Fleetmaster	Fleetol Multilite 10W/30	
ESSO	Esso Uniflo 15W/50	Esso Uniflo 10W/40	Esso Uniflo 5W/40	Essolube HDX Plus 20W/50 Esso Uniflo 15W/50	Essolube HDX Plus 10W/30 Esso Uniflo 10W/40	Essolube MDX Plus 10W/30 Esso Uniflo 5W/40
MOBIL	Mobiloil Super 15W/50	Mobiloil SHC 10W/50	Mobiloil 1 5W/20 Mobiloil 5W/20	Mobil Delvac Super 15W/40 Delvac Special 20W/50	Mobil Delvac Special 10W/30	Mobiloil 5W/20
PETROFINA	Fina Supergrade Motor Oil 20W/50	Fina Supergrade Motor Oil 10W/40		Fina Delta Multigrade 20W/50	Fina Delta Multigrade 10W/30	
SHELL	Shell Super Motor Oil U.K. 20W/50 Europe 15W/50	Shell Super Motor Oil 10W/40 (Norway, Sweden, Canada) 10W/50 (Rest of Europe, U.S.A.)	Shell Super Motor Oil 5W/40 (Finland) 5W/30 (Canada)	Rotella SX Rotella TX 20W/40 Rotella SX 20W/20 (Sweden)	Rotella TX 10W/30 Rotella SX 10W/20 (Sweden)	Rotella TX 5W/20 (Finland, Canada)
TEXACO	Texaco URSA Oil LA 15W/40			Eurotex Motor Oil HD 20W/50	Eurotex Motor Oil HD 10W/30	

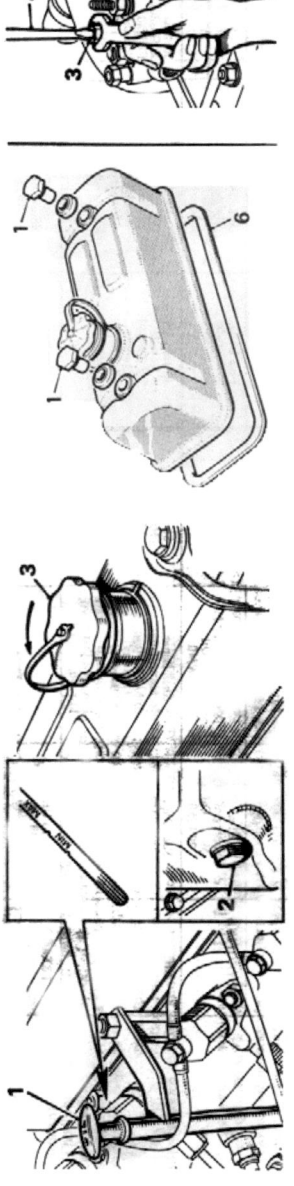

ENGINE

Lubrication

Checking oil level
1 Maintain the level between the 'MIN' and 'MAX' mark on the dipstick.

Draining and refilling
2 Drain the oil while the engine is warm: check the drain plug copper washer before refitting.
3 Refill with the correct quantity and grade of oil. Run the engine for a short while, then allow it to stand for a few minutes before re-checking the level.

Disposable cartridge filter renewal
4 Unscrew the old cartridge with a tourniquet type wrench; a quantity of oil will be released. Discard the cartridge and seal (5).
5 Wet the new seal with engine oil and ensure that it is located correctly in its groove in the new cartridge.
6 Screw the new cartridge to the filter head, using hand force only.
7 Start the engine and check the filter for leaks. Stop the engine, and re-check the oil level after waiting for a few minutes.

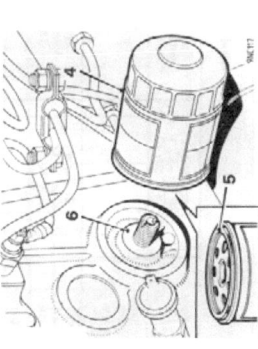

Valve rocker adjustment
1 Remove the rocker cover.
2 Check the clearance between the valve rocker arms and valve stems with a feeler gauge.
Clearance: see 'ENGINE TUNING DATA'.
The gauge should be a sliding fit when the engine is cold.
Check the clearance of each valve in the following order:
Check No. 1 valve with No. 8 fully open.
"   "   3   "   "   "   6   "   "
"   "   5   "   "   "   4   "   "
"   "   2   "   "   "   7   "   "
"   "   8   "   "   "   1   "   "
"   "   6   "   "   "   3   "   "
"   "   4   "   "   "   5   "   "
"   "   7   "   "   "   2   "   "

3 Slacken the locknut.
4 Rotate screw, clockwise to decrease or anti-clockwise to increase the clearance.
Retighten the locknut when the clearance is correct, holding the screw against rotation.
Refit the rocker cover checking that the gasket is serviceable.

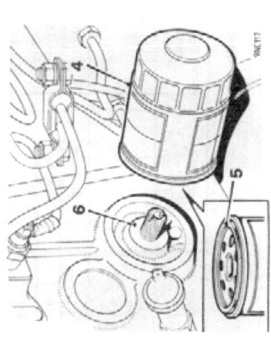

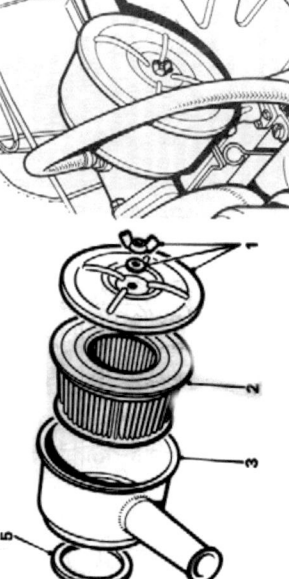

DRIVE BELT TENSION

Checking
1 Use one of the following methods of checking the belt tension:

a Use a torque spanner and apply a load of 14.9 to 15.6 Nm (1.5 to 1.6 kgf m, 11.0 to 11.5 lbf ft) in a clockwise direction to the alternator pulley retaining nut. If the belt tension is correct the belt will slip at this torque loading.

b Apply a load of 33.4 to 36.4 N (3.3 to 3.6 kgf, 7.5 to 8.2 lbf) at right angles to the belt midway between pulleys. The belt should deflect 6 mm (0.25 m). It is important that the belt tension is set correctly.

NOTE: Fit a new belt with a moderate degree of tension, run the engine for five minutes at 1000 rev/min, stop the engine then set the belt to the correct tension.

Adjusting
2 Slacken the alternator securing bolts.
3 Slacken the bolt securing the adjusting link to the alternator.
4 Slacken the adjusting link to engine securing nut.
5 Move the alternator to the required position; avoid over-tightening. Apply any leverage necessary to the alternator drive end bracket only, using a wood or soft metal lever.
6 Tighten the securing nuts and bolts.

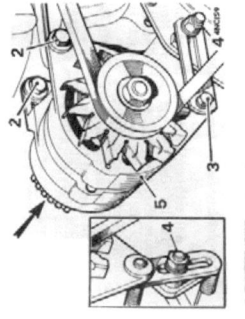

FUEL SYSTEM

Air cleaner elements

Renew the air cleaner element. In dusty operating conditions the element may require changing more frequently than recommended.

Removing
1 Unscrew the wing nut, remove the fibre washer and withdraw the cover.
2 Withdraw and discard the element.
3 Clean the interior of the container.

Refitting
4 Fit the element.
5 Check that the sealing ring is in good condition.
6 Refit the cover, fibre washer and nut.

SERVICE OPERATIONS – Summary

Every 150 hours
Change engine oil

Operation	Every 300 hours	Every 600 hours
Check/adjust drive belt tension	X	X
Check/adjust valve clearances	X	X
Renew main fuel filter element	X	X
Change engine oil and filter element		X
Test injectors for spray		X
Remove heater plugs and clean carbon from each plug orifice in cylinder head – check heater plug operation		X
Renew oil filler cap		X
Clean/renew air filter element	X	X
Check governor settings		X
Retorque cylinder head nuts		X

NOTE: More frequent air cleaner element servicing may be necessary in dirty/dusty conditions.

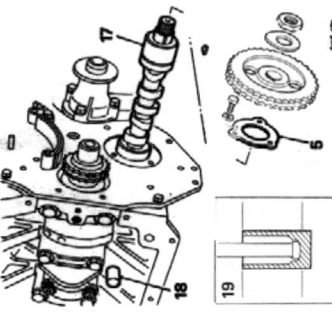

FUEL INJECTION PUMP HUB

Remove and refit 12.10.26
Fuel injection pump gear 1 to 5 and 12 to 18 12.10.25

Removing
1. Remove the timing chain, see 12.65.14.
2. Remove the injection pump, see 19.30.07.
3. Remove the four bolts from the injection pump driving flange.
4. Withdraw the driving flange and collect the two locating half plates.
5. Withdraw the injection pump gear.
6. Remove the injection pump drive oil feed pipe.
7. Remove the countersunk screw from the injection pump hub.
8. Remove the upper bolt from the chain vibration damper.
9. Remove the injection pump hub.
10. Remove the hub gasket.
11. Remove the oil pipe union from the hub.

Refitting
12. Reverse the procedure in 5 to 11.
13. Ensure that the circlip is correctly located in its groove in the splined bore of the injection pump driving flange.
14. Fit one of the locating half plates to its groove in the injection pump hub, and position it by inserting a ⅜ in (5.5 mm) peg through the timing hole in the locating plate and into the timing hole in the gear.
15. Fit the second locating half plate and then fit the driving flange, engaging the driving flange timing hole with the peg.
16. Fit and tighten the driving flange bolts to 10 lbf ft (1.4 kgf m, 14 Nm); ensure that the peg can be withdrawn from the timing hole and lock the bolts with their lockplates.
17. Fit the timing chain, see 12.65.14, but do not connect the battery.
18. Fit the injection pump, see 19.30.07.

OIL PUMP DRIVE SHAFT

Remove and refit 12.10.30
Oil pump 12.60.26
Oil pick-up strainer 12.60.20

Removing
1. Disconnect the battery.
2. Drain the sump.
3. Disconnect the oil cooler pipe from the L.H. side of the crankcase.
4. Release the oil pipe clip from the gearbox mounting plate and move the oil pipe aside.
5. Remove the sump.
6. Remove the oil strainer and gasket.
7. Remove the three oil pump securing nuts.
8. Withdraw the oil pump and its drive shaft.
9. Withdraw the drive shaft from the oil pump.
10. Remove the oil pump gasket.

Refitting
11. Reverse the procedure in 1 to 10, tightening the oil pump securing nuts to 16 lbf ft (2.2 kgf m, 22 Nm).

TAPPETS

Remove and refit 12.29.57
Camshaft 1 to 17 and 20 to 32 12.13.02

Service tool: 18G 694

Removing
1. Disconnect the battery.
2. Drain the sump.
3. Remove the engine.
4. Remove the timing chain and the camshaft gear, see 12.65.12.
5. Remove the camshaft locating plate.
6. Remove the fuel lift pump.
7. Remove the rocker cover and gasket.
8. Slacken evenly and remove the eight nuts retaining the rocker shaft brackets.
9. Remove the locking plate from the rocker shaft rear bracket.
10. Remove the rocker shaft assembly and the shim under each centre bracket.
11. Withdraw the push-rods and retain their order for refitting.

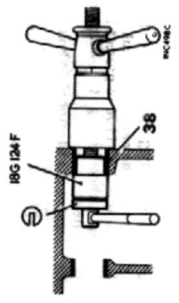

12. Lay the engine on its side with the cylinder head slightly downwards.
13. Withdraw the dipstick.
14. Remove the sump.
15. Remove the oil pump and its drive shaft.
16. Rotate the camshaft to position all the tappets away from their cams.
17. Withdraw the camshaft.
18. Withdraw the tappets and retain their order for refitting.

Refitting
19. Fit the tappets with their open ends towards the cylinder head.
20. Fit the camshaft.
21. Fit the oil pump and its drive shaft, tightening the retaining nuts to 16 lbf ft (2.2 kgf m, 22 Nm)
22. Fit the sump.
23. Fit the dipstick.
24. Place the engine in an upright position.
25. Fit the push-rods.
26. Fit the rocker shaft assembly, noting:
    a. Ensure that the shim is fitted under both centre brackets.
    b. Fit the locking plate to the rear bracket.
    c. Tighten the cylinder head nuts to 75 lbf ft (10.4 kgf m, 102 Nm) in the sequence shown, using tool 18G 694 to reach the centre row. Tighten the rocker bracket nuts to 25 lbf ft (3.5 kgf m, 34 Nm).
    d. Fit the fuel lift pump.
27. Fit the fuel lift pump.
28. Fit the camshaft locating plate.
29. Fit the camshaft gear, timing chain, and timing gear cover, see 12.65.1.2.
    NOTE: Do not leave the crankshaft pulley in position.
30. Adjust the valve rocker clearance, see 12.29.48.
31. Fit the rocker cover and its gasket.
32. Fit the engine.
33. Run the engine for a minimum of 5 miles, 8 km or 15 mins and on return slacken the cylinder head nuts approximately ¼ of a turn in the sequence shown before retightening them to 75 lbf ft (10.4 kgf m, 102 Nm) in the sequence shown. Check the valve rocker clearances.

complete with injection pump, front mounting brackets, chain tensioner stop-pin, front and chain tensioner shoe.
18. Remove the fuel lift pump.
19. Withdraw the dipstick.
20. Release the dipstick tube from the cylinder head nut and withdraw the tube from the crankcase.
21. Disconnect and remove No. 1 heater plug.
22. Remove the rocker cover and gasket.
23. Remove the rocker shaft assembly, noting the locking plate on the rear bracket and the shim under each centre bracket.
24. Withdraw the push-rods, retaining their order for refitting.
25. Remove the cylinder head nuts.
26. Lift off the cylinder head.
    NOTE: The combustion chamber inserts (if fitted) may drop out of the cylinder head as it is lifted; they MUST be refitted in their original positions.
27. Remove the cylinder head gasket.
28. Lay the engine on its side with the cylinder head face slightly downwards.
29. Remove the sump.
30. Remove the oil pump and its drive shaft.
31. Remove the big-end bearing caps and bearing halves.
32. Remove the main bearing caps and bearing halves, using tools 18G 284, 18G 284 A, and 18G 284 AC.
33. Lift out the crankshaft and remove the bearing and thrust washer halves.
34. Withdraw the connecting rod and piston assemblies.
35. Rotate the camshaft to position all the tappets away from their cams.
36. Withdraw the camshaft.
37. Withdraw the tappets and retain their order for refitting.
38. Remove the camshaft front bearing liner, using tools 18G 124 A and 18G 124 F as shown.
39. Remove the camshaft rear bearing liner, using tools 18G 124 A and 18G 124 B as shown.
40. Remove the camshaft centre bearing liner, using tools 18G 124 A, 18G 124 C, and 18G 124 H as shown.

continued

CAMSHAFT BEARINGS —[2]**

Remove and refit 12.13.13

Service tools: 18G 55 A, 18G 123 A, 18G 123 B, 18G 123 E, 18G 123 F, 18G 123 L, 18G 123 T, 18G 123 AB, 18G 123 AC, 18G 123 AD, 18G 124 A, 18G 124 B, 18G 124 C, 18G 124 F, 18G 124 H, 18G 134, 18G 134 CQ, 18G 284, 18G 284 A, 18G 284 AC, 18G 694, 18G 1108, 18G 1195

Removing
1. Disconnect the battery.
2. Drain the sump.
3. Remove the engine.
4. Remove the clutch assembly.
5. Remove the flywheel.
6. Remove the crankshaft rear oil seal retainer.
7. Remove the bolts securing the gearbox adaptor plate and pull the adaptor plate off its two locating dowels.
8. Remove the two adaptor plate gaskets.
9. Remove the alternator.
10. Remove the high-pressure pipes from the injectors and pump.
11. Remove the injection pump drive oil feed pipe.
12. Remove the timing chain and the camshaft gear, see 12.65.12.
13. Remove the camshaft locating plate.
14. Remove the chain vibration damper.
15. Remove the bolt securing each front mounting bracket to the crankcase.
16. Remove the two bolts securing the front mounting plate to the crankcase.
17. Lift off the front mounting plate,

** [1] [2] see page 7

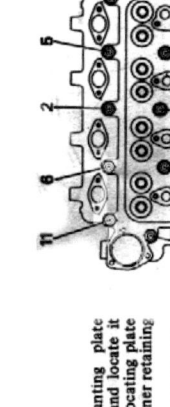

Refitting
NOTE: When fitting each new bearing liner ensure that its oil holes are lined up with those in the crankcase.

41. Fit a new camshaft front bearing liner, using tools 18G 124 A and 18G 124 F as shown.
42. Fit a new camshaft rear bearing liner, using tools 18G 124 A and 18G 124 B as shown.
43. Fit a new camshaft centre bearing liner, using tools 18G 124 A, 18G 124 C, and 18G 124 H as shown.

NOTE: Lightly lubricate the arbor before assembling the cutters and pilots to it. Feed the reamers very slowly and keep the cutters dry. Keep the cutter flutes clear of swarf during reaming.

44. Ream the front and rear bearing liners using tools 18G 123 A, 18G 123 L, 18G 123 E (in position '10' on the arbor), 18G 123 B (in position '6' on the arbor), and 18G 123 AC as shown.
45. Ream the centre bearing liner, using tools 18G 123 A, 18G 123 T, 18G 123 F (in position '9' on the arbor) and 18G 123 AD as shown.
46. Ensure that the oil holes of the bearing liners are still lined up with those in the crankcase.
47. Thoroughly clean all swarf from the cylinder block and crankcase.
48. Fit the tappets with their open ends towards the cylinder head.
49. Fit the camshaft.
50. Fit the connecting rod and piston assemblies with the combustion cavities on the R.H. side of the engine, using tool 18G 55 A.
51. Fit the crankshaft main bearings, and thrust washers (grooved side towards the crankshaft) to the crankcase.
52. Fit the main bearing caps, noting:
   a Caps Nos. 2 and 4 are each stamped with their number.
   b Fit caps 2, 3 and 4 with the cast word 'FRONT' towards the front of the engine.
   c Using a straight-edge, align the front and rear bearing caps with the front and rear faces of the crankcase.
   d Tighten the main bearing bolts to 75 lbf ft (10.4 kgf m, 102 Nm).
53. Check the crankshaft end-float against the figure in DATA, and fit alternative thrust washers if necessary.
54. Fit the big-end bearings and caps, ensuring that the connecting rod and cap markings are aligned.
55. Tighten the big-end nuts to 35 lbf ft (4.8 kgf m, 47 Nm).
56. Fit the oil pump and its drive shaft, tightening the retaining nuts to 16 lbf ft (2.2 kgf m, 22 Nm).
57. Soak the cork sealing strips in engine oil, then fit them to the front and rear main bearing caps.
58. Fit the sump.
59. Position the front mounting plate assembly on the engine and locate it by fitting the camshaft locating plate bolts and the chain tensioner retaining screw.
60. Fit the two bolts to secure the mounting plate to the crankcase.
61. Fit the two bolts to secure both front mounting brackets to the crankcase.
62. Fit the chain vibration damper.
63. Fit the camshaft locating plate.
64. Fit the camshaft gear, timing chain, and timing gear cover, see 12.65.12.
65. Reverse the procedure in 18 to 27, noting:
   a Fit the cylinder head gasket with the face marked 'TOP' uppermost.
   b Ensure that the combustion chamber inserts (if fitted) are flush with the cylinder head face.
   c Leave the cylinder head assembly finger tight until the rocker shaft assembly has been fitted.
   d Tighten the cylinder head nuts to 75 lbf ft (10.4 kgf m, 102 Nm) in the sequence shown, using tool 18G 694 to reach the centre row.
   e Tighten the rocker bracket nuts to 25 lbf ft (3.5 kgf m, 34 Nm).
   f Adjust the valve rocker clearance, see 12.29.48.
   g Apply Loctite to the bottom of the dipstick tube.
66. Reverse the procedure in 4 to 11, noting:
   a Use tools 18G 134 and 18G 134 CQ to fit the new rear oil seal.
   b Use tool 18G 1108 to protect the seal when fitting the adaptor plate.
   c Tighten the adaptor plate bolts to 30 lbf ft (4.2 kgf m, 41 Nm).
   NOTE: Fit the two longer bolts in the two top holes.

d   Tighten the oil seal retainer bolts to 20 lbf ft (2,8 kgf m, 27 Nm).
e   Tighten the flywheel bolts to 40 lbf ft (5,5 kgf m, 54 Nm).
f   Fit the clutch driven plate with the 'FLYWHEEL SIDE' marking towards the flywheel, using tool 18G 1195 to centralise the driven plate.
67 Fit the engine.

DATA
Crankshaft end-float . . . . . . 0.001 to 0.0055 in (0.03 to 0.14 mm)
Thrust washer thicknesses .   0.0885 to 0.0905 in (2.25 to 2.30 mm),
                                0.091 to 0.093 in (2.31 to 2.36 mm) and
                                0.0935 to 0.0955 in (2.37 to 2.43 mm)

68 Run the engine for a minimum of 5 miles, 8 km or 15 mins and on return slacken the cylinder head nuts approximately ¼ of a turn in the sequence shown before retightening them to 75 lbf ft (10,4 kgf m, 102 Nm) in the sequence shown. Check the valve rocker clearances.

CONNECTING RODS AND PISTONS

Remove and refit   12.17.01
Service tool: 18G 55 A

Removing
1   Disconnect the battery.
2   Drain the sump.
3   Drain the cooling system.
4   Remove the cylinder head gasket, see 12.29.02.
5   Disconnect the oil cooler pipe from the L.H. side of the crankcase.
6   Release the oil cooler pipe clip from the gearbox mounting plate and move the oil pipe aside.
7   Remove the sump.
8   Remove the big-end nuts.
9   Remove the big-end caps and bearing halves.
10 Withdraw the connecting rod and piston assemblies.
11 Mark the pistons and connecting rods for reassembly.
12 Remove the circlips and the gudgeon pins and separate the pistons from the connecting rods.

Refitting
13 Reverse the procedure in 8 to 12, noting:
  a Assemble the pistons to the connecting rods with the combustion cavities on the oil hole side of the connecting rods.
  b If new piston rings are being used ensure that the ring gaps are correct, see 12.17.10.
  c Use tool 18G 55 A to compress the piston rings.
  d Fit the connecting rod and piston assemblies with the combustion cavities on the R.H. side of the engine.
14 If the connecting rods or piston(s) have been renewed, rotate the crankshaft and measure the amount by which each piston stands proud of the cylinder block face at T.D.C.
15 If piston stand-proud is outside the limits given in DATA, fit suitable alternative piston(s) from the range available.
    NOTE: It is not necessary for the pistons in an engine to be of the same height grade.
16 Tighten the big-end nuts to 35 lbf ft (4,8 kgf m, 47 Nm).
17 Reverse the procedure in 1 to 7.

DATA
Piston stand-proud . . . . . .   0.013 to 0.021 in (0.33 to 0.53 mm)
Piston compression height   1.977 to 1.979 in (50,22 to 50,27 mm)

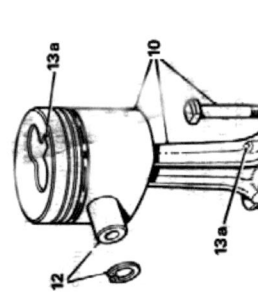

CONNECTING RODS AND PISTONS

Overhaul 12.17.10
Connecting rods 1 to 5 and 10 to 12
Pistons 1 to 9 and 12

1. Disconnect the battery.
2. Drain the sump.
3. Drain the cooling system.
4. Remove the cylinder head gasket, see 12.29.02.
5. Remove and separate the connecting rods and pistons, see 12.17.01.
6. Remove the rings from the pistons.
7. Check the piston ring gaps, in an unworn part of the cylinder bore, against the figures in DATA. If necessary, increase the gap(s) by filing the end of the ring(s).
8. Fit the piston rings, noting:
   a. Fit the oil control ring expander spring first, ensuring that the latch pin enters both ends of the spring.
   b. Fit the oil control ring with its gap 180° from the expander latch pin.
   c. Fit the second ring with the word 'TOP' uppermost.
9. Check the piston ring groove clearance against the figures in DATA.
10. Check the gudgeon pin clearance in the connecting rod bush (see DATA). If the clearance is excessive, renew the bush, noting:
    a. Position the bush with its hole and oil grooves towards the top.
    b. Finish-ream the bush to the dimension given in DATA.
11. Ensure that the connecting rod alignment is within the figure given in DATA.
12. Reverse the procedure in 1 to 5.

DATA

Connecting rod alignment
Maximum out-of-parallel of big-end and little-end .... 0.004 in per inch (0.004 cm per cm) effective mandrel length

Connecting rod bush
Clearance on gudgeon pin .... 0.0002 to 0.0009 in (0.02 to 0.04 mm)
Inside diameter (reamed after fitting) 1.0002 to 1.0007 in (25.41 to 25.42 mm)

Piston rings
Fitted gap:
  Top compression .... 0.012 to 0.017 in (0.30 to 0.43 mm)
  Second compression .... 0.009 to 0.014 in (0.23 to 0.35 mm)
  Oil control .... 0.012 to 0.017 in (0.30 to 0.43 mm)
Ring to groove clearance:
  Top compression .... 0.0025 to 0.0045 in (0.06 to 0.11 mm)
  Second compression .... 0.0015 to 0.0035 in (0.04 to 0.09 mm)
  Oil control .... 0.0015 to 0.0035 in (0.04 to 0.09 mm)

CRANKSHAFT REAR OIL SEAL

Remove and refit 12.21.20
Gearbox adaptor plate 12.53.03
Flywheel 1 to 8 and 15 12.53.07

Service tools: 18G 134, 18G 134 CQ, 18G 1108

Removing
1. Disconnect the battery.
2. Remove the gearbox.
3. Remove the clutch assembly, see 33.10.01.
4. Remove the flywheel securing bolts.
5. Lift off the flywheel.
6. Remove the oil seal retainer.
7. Remove the 10 bolts securing the gearbox adaptor plate.
8. Pull the adaptor plate off its two locating dowels.
9. Remove the two adaptor plate gaskets.
10. Remove the oil seal from the adaptor plate.

Refitting
11. Fit the new oil seal flush with the rear face of the adaptor plate, using tools 18G 134 and 18G 134 CQ.
12. Reverse the procedure in 1 to 10, noting:
    a. Use tool 18G 1108 to protect the oil seal when fitting the adaptor plate.
    b. Tighten the adaptor plate bolts to 30 lbf ft (4.2 kgf m, 41 Nm).
       NOTE: Fit the two longer bolts in the two top holes.
    c. Tighten the oil seal retainer bolts to 20 lbf ft (2.8 kgf m, 27 Nm).
    d. Tighten the flywheel bolts to 40 lbf ft (5.5 kgf m, 54 Nm).

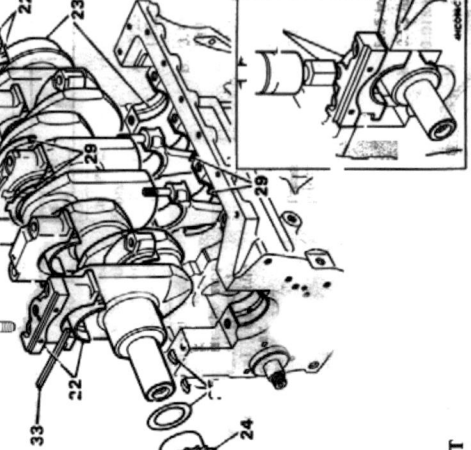

CRANKSHAFT END-FLOAT

Check and adjust 12.21.26

1. Disconnect the battery.
2. Check the crankshaft end-float using a dial gauge against the crankshaft pulley bolt. If end-float is outside the limits given in DATA, change the thrust washers as described in the following paragraphs.
3. Drain the sump.
4. Release the oil pipe clip from the gearbox mountint plate and move the oil pipe aside.
5. Remove the sump.
6. Remove the oil pump and its drive shaft.
7. Remove the two bolts from the centre main bearing cap.
8. Remove the centre main bearing cap.
9. Remove the bottom halves of the thrust washers from the cap or crankshaft.
10. Slide the upper halves of the thrust washers around the crank and remove them.
11. Select a set of thrust washers to give the correct end-float (see DATA).
12. Reverse the procedure in 3 to 10, noting:
   a Fit the thrust washers with their grooved sides towards the crankshaft.
   b Fit the main bearing cap with the 'FRONT' mark towards the front of the engine.

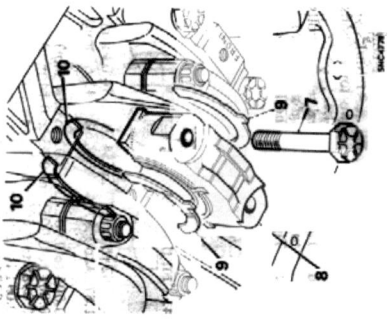

c Tighten the main bearing cap bolts to 75 lbf ft (10.4 kgf m, 102 Nm).
d Ensure that the end-float is correct after tightening the main bearing cap bolts.
e Tighten the oil pump securing nuts to 16 lbf ft (2.2 kgf m, 22 Nm).
13 Connect the battery.

DATA
Crankshaft end-float ..... 0.001 to 0.0055 in (0.03 to 0.14 mm)
Thrust washer thicknesses 0.0885 to 0.0905 in (2.25 to 2.30 mm)
0.091 to 0.093 in (2.31 to 2.36 mm) and
0.0935 to 0.0955 in (2.37 to 2.43 mm)

CRANKSHAFT

Remove and refit 12.21.33

Service tools: 18G 134, 18G 134 CQ, 18G 284, 18G 284 AC, 18G 1108, 18G 1195

Removing
1. Disconnect the battery.
2. Drain the sump.
3. Remove the engine.
4. Remove the clutch assembly.
5. Remove the flywheel.
6. Remove the crankshaft rear oil seal retainer.
7. Remove the bolts securing the gearbox adaptor plate and pull the adaptor plate off its two locating dowels.
8. Remove the two adaptor plate gaskets.
9. Remove the alternator.
10. Disconnect the high-pressure pipes from the injectors.
11. Remove the injection pump drive oil feed pipe.
12. Remove the timing chain and the camshaft gear, see 12.65.12.
13. Remove the camshaft locating plate.
14. Remove the chain vibration damper.
15. Remove the bolt securing each front mounting bracket to the crankcase.
16. Remove the two bolts securing the front mounting plate to the crankcase.
17. Lift off the front mounting plate, complete with injection pump, front mounting brackets, chain tensioner stop-pin, and chain tensioner shoe.
18. Withdraw the dipstick.
19. Remove the sump.

continued

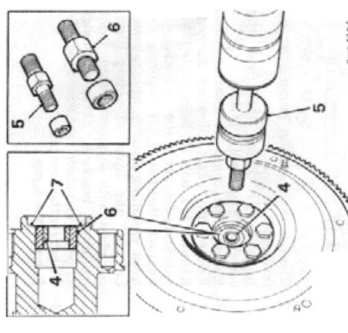

20 Remove the oil pump and its drive shaft.
21 Remove the big-end bearing caps and bearing halves.
   NOTE: If the crankshaft has to be rotated, be careful not to apply any force which could cause damage if a piston touches a valve.
22 Remove the main bearing caps and bearing halves, using tools 18G 284 and 18G 284 AC on the front and rear caps if necessary.
23 Lift out the crankshaft and remove the bearing and thrust washer halves.
24 Remove the crankshaft gear.
25 Remove the crankshaft keys and lift off the shim(s).

Refitting
26 Fit the shim(s), keys and gear to the crankshaft.
27 Fit the crankshaft, main bearings, and thrust washers (grooved side towards the crankshaft) to the crankcase.
28 Fit the main bearing caps, noting:
   a Caps Nos. 2 and 4 are each stamped with their number.
   b Fit caps 2, 3, and 4 with the cast word 'FRONT' towards the front of the engine.
   c Using a straight-edge, align the front and rear faces of the front and rear bearing caps with the front and rear faces of the crankcase.
   d Tighten the main bearing bolts to 75 lbf ft (10.4 kgf m, 102 Nm).
29 Check the crankshaft end-float against the figure in DATA, and fit alternative thrust washers if necessary.
30 Fit the big-end bearings and caps, ensuring that the connecting rod and cap markings are aligned.
31 Tighten the big-end nuts to 35 lbf ft (4.8 kgf m, 47 Nm).

32 Fit the oil pump and its drive shaft, tightening the retaining nuts to 16 lbf ft (2.2 kgf m, 22 Nm).
33 Soak the cork sealing strips in engine oil, then fit them to the front and rear main bearing caps.
34 Fit the sump.
35 Fit the dipstick.
36 Position the front mounting plate assembly on the engine and locate it by fitting the camshaft locating plate bolts and the chain tensioner retaining screw.
37 Fit the two bolts to secure the front mountig plate to the crankcase.
38 Fit the two bolts to secure both front mounting plate to the crankcase.
39 Fit the chain vibration damper.
40 Fit the camshaft locating plate.
41 Fit the camshaft gear, timing chain, and timing gear cover, see 12.65.12.
   NOTE: Do not leave the crankshaft pulley in position.
42 Reverse the procedure in 4 to 11, noting:
   a Use tools 18G 134 and 18G 134 CQ to fit the new rear oil seal.
   b Use tool 18G 1108 to protect the seal when fitting the adaptor plate.
   c Tighten the adaptor plate bolts to 30 lbf ft (4.2 kgf m, 41 Nm).
      NOTE: Fit the two longer bolts in the two top holes.
   d Tighten the oil seal retainer bolts to 20 lbf ft (2.8 kgf m, 27 Nm).
   e Tighten the flywheel bolts to 40 lbf ft (5.5 kgf m, 54 Nm).
   f Fit the clutch driven plate with the 'FLYWHEEL SIDE' marking towards the flywheel, using tool 18G 1195 to centralize the driven plate.
43 Fit the engine.

CRANKSHAFT SPIGOT BUSH 12.21.45
Remove and refit
Service tools: 18G 284, 18G 284 AAF

Removing
1 Disconnect the battery.
2 Remove the gearbox, see 37.20.01.
3 Remove the clutch assembly, see 33.10.01.
4 Cut a thread in the spigot bush, using a ⅝ in U.N.F. tap.
5 Remove the bush, using tool 18G 284 and the appropriate adaptor 18G 284 AAF.
6 If the spigot bush is a composite type, remove the larger (steel) bush by repeating operations 4 and 5 using a ⅞ in B.S.P. threadform tap.

Refitting
7 Fit the new spigot bush flush with the crankshaft counterbore.
8 Reverse the procedure in 1 to 3.

DATA
Main journal diameter .... 2.1262 to 2.1270 in (54.01 to 54.03 mm)
Crankpin diameter .... 1.8759 to 1.8764 in (47.64 to 47.65 mm)
Clearance in bearings (journals and crankpin) .... 0.001 to 0.0027 in (0.03 to 0.07 mm)
                                     0.001 to 0.0055 in (0.03 to 0.14 mm)
Crankshaft end-float .... 0.0885 to 0.0905 in (2.25 to 2.30 mm)
                                     0.091 to 0.093 in (2.31 to 2.36 mm) and
Thrust washer thicknesses .... 0.0935 to 0.0955 in (2.37 to 2.43 mm)

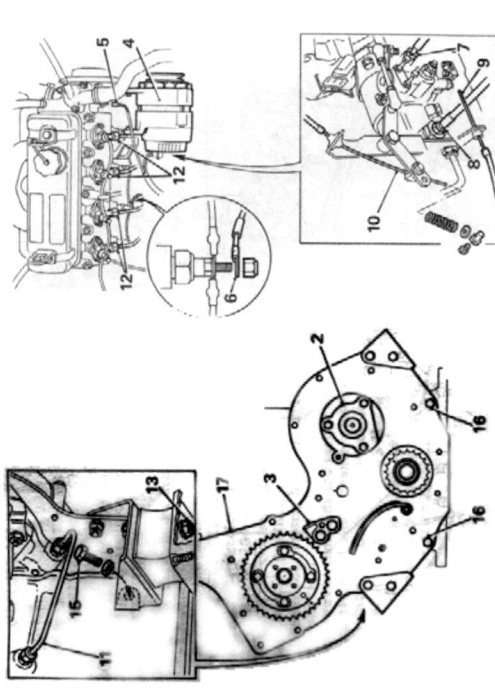

Pressing-out pilot:	A. 3.25 $^{-0.005}_{-0.011}$ (82.55 $^{-0.00}_{-0.28}$ mm)
	B. 3.157 $^{+0.005}_{+0.013}$ (80.19 $^{+0.13}_{+0.33}$ mm)
	C. 1.75 in (44.45 mm)
	D. 0.75 in (19 mm)
	F. ¾ in B.S.W. thread
	G. 3.625 in (92.07 mm)
	H. 3.312 in (84.14 mm)
	3.133 $^{+0.005}_{-0.013}$ in (79.58 $^{+0.13}_{-0.33}$ mm)
	J. 1.25 in (31.75 mm)
	K. 0.75 in (19 mm)
	L. 0.015 in (0.38 mm)
Pressing-in pilot:	M. 14.50 in (36.83 cm)
	N. 0.875 in (22.22 mm)
	P. 0.625 in (15.87 mm)
	Q. 0.625 in (15.87 mm)
	R. Two flats 1 in (25.4 mm) across
	S. ¾ in B.S.W. thread
Pilot extension:	T. 1.25 in (31.75 mm)

18 Remove the front mounting plate gasket.

Refitting
19 Fit the front mounting plate gasket.
20 Position the front mounting plate assembly on the engine and locate it by fitting the camshaft locating plate bolts and the chain tensioner retaining screw.
21 Reverse the procedure in 1 to 16, noting:
  a With the throttle cable connected to the inner hole in the bell-crank lever, ensure that the injection pump throttle lever is operated through its full range of movement by the throttle pedal.
  b When the stop control cable is connected, ensure that the stop control has sufficient travel to permit removal of the master/starter switch key.
22 Bleed the fuel system, see 19.50.07.

CYLINDER LINERS

Remove and refit 12.25.26

NOTE: If the condition of the cylinder bores is such that they cannot be cleaned up to accept oversize pistons, dry cylinder liners can be fitted (see DATA).
Pilots should be made to the dimensions given, from case-hardening steel and case-hardened.
The pilot extension should be made from 55-ton hardening and tempering steel, hardened in oil, and then tempered at 550°C (1020°F).

DATA

Cylinder block
Bore: Standard .... 3.1595 to 3.1606 in (80.25 to 80.28 mm)
Oversize maximum (without cylinder liner) .... 0.040 in (1.02 mm)
To accept cylinder liner ... 3.2615 to 3.2620 in (82.84 to 82.86 mm)

Cylinder liners
Outside diameter
Bore: Standard (machined after fitting) 3.2645 to 3.2660 in (82.92 to 82.96 mm)
3.1595 to 3.1606 in (80.25 to 80.28 mm)
Oversize (maximum) .... 0.020 in (0.51 mm)

10 Disconnect the throttle cable from the injection pump bracket and bell-crank lever.
11 Remove the injection pump drive oil feed pipe.
12 Disconnect the high-pressure pipes from the injectors.
13 Remove the nuts and washers from the underside of both engine front mountings.
14 Raise the engine sufficiently to clear the lower studs in the front mountings.
15 Remove the bolt securing each front mounting bracket to the crankcase.
16 Remove the two bolts and washers securing the front mounting plate to the crankcase.
17 Lift off the front mounting plate, complete with injection pump, front mountings, chain tensioner stop-pin, and chain tensioner shoe.

ENGINE FRONT MOUNTING PLATE GASKET

Remove and refit 12.25.10

Removing
1 Remove the timing chain and the camshaft gear, see 12.65.12.
2 Remove the camshaft locating plate.
3 Remove the chain vibration damper.
4 Remove the alternator.
5 Disconnect the thermal transmitter and move the wiring harness aside.
6 Disconnect the supply lead from the heater plugs.
7 Disconnect the fuel return pipe from the injection pump.
8 Disconnect the fuel supply pipe from the injection pump.
9 Disconnect the stop control cable from the injection pump.

12.29.02

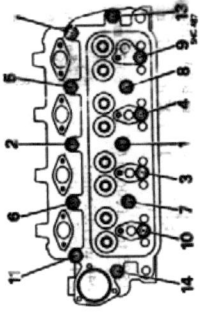

Removing

1. Disconnect the battery.
2. Drain the cooling system.
3. Disconnect both hoses from the water outlet elbow.
4. Disconnect the breather hose from the cylinder side cover.
5. Remove the air cleaner and elbow.
6. Remove the clamp and separate the exhaust pipe from the manifold.
7. Disconnect the lead from the thermal transmitter.
8. Disconnect the supply lead from the heater plugs.
9. Disconnect the spill rail and return pipe from the injectors and lay the spill rail aside.
10. Remove Nos. 3 and 4 injector pipes.
11. Remove Nos. 1 and 2 injector pipes.
12. Remove the oil dipstick.
13. Release the dipstick tube from the cylinder head nut and withdraw the tube from the crankcase.
14. Disconnect and remove No. 1 heater plug.
15. Remove the rocker cover and gasket.
16. Remove the rocker shaft assembly, noting the locking plate on the rear bracket and the shim under each centre bracket.
17. Withdraw the push-rods, retaining their order for refitting.
18. Remove the cylinder head nuts.
19. Lift off the cylinder head.
    NOTE: The combustion chamber inserts (if fitted) may drop out of the cylinder head as it is lifted; they MUST be refitted in their original positions.
20. Remove the cylinder head gasket.

Refitting

21. Reverse the procedure in 1 to 20, noting:
    a. Fit the cylinder head gasket with the face marked 'TOP' uppermost.
    b. Ensure that the combustion chamber inserts (if fitted) are flush with the cylinder head face.
    c. Leave the cylinder head nuts finger tight until the rocker shaft assembly has been fitted.
    d. Tighten the cylinder head nuts to 75 lbf ft (10.4 kgf m, 102 Nm) in the sequence shown, using tool 18G 694 to reach the centre row. Tighten the rocker brackets nuts to 25 lbf ft (3.5 kgf m, 34 Nm).
    e. Adjust the valve rocker clearance, see 12.29.48.
    f. Bleed the fuel system, see 19.50.05.
    g. Apply Loctite to the bottom of the dipstick tube.
22. Run the engine for a minimum of 5 miles, 8 km or 15 mins and on return slacken the cylinder head nuts approximately ¼ of a turn in the sequence shown before retightening them to 75 lbf ft (10.4 kgf m, 102 Nm) in the sequence shown. Check the valve rocker clearances.

CYLINDER HEAD

Overhaul   12.29.19

Service tools: 18G 27 or MS 76, 18G 29, 18G 45 (18G 167, 18G 167 A and 18G 167 B) or MS 204, 18G 167 C (18G 174, 18G 174 A and 18G 174 B) or MS 621, 18G 174 D or MS 150-8.5, 18G 284, 18G 284 P

1. Remove the cylinder head gasket, see 12.29.02.
2. Remove the three remaining heater plugs from the cylinder head.
3. Remove the injectors, using tools 18G 284, and 18G 284 P.
4. Remove the two sealing washers from each injector position.
5. Remove the heater hose from the cylinder head.
6. Remove the manifolds and gasket.
7. Mark the combustion chamber inserts for refitting in their original positions.
8. Remove the combustion chamber inserts, if necessary using a soft drift through the injector holes.
9. Push out the injector heat shields and their sealing washers.
10. Remove the water outlet elbow and its gasket.
11. Lift out the thermostat.
12. Remove the valves and their components, using tool 18G 45.
    NOTE: Seals are fitted to the inlet valve guides.
13. If the valve guides are worn (see DATA), press them out in the direction of the valve seats.
14. To fit new valve guides, press them in from the top of the cylinder head until they protrude by the amount stated in DATA. Protrusion is measured from the top of the valve guide to the bottom of the counter bore for the valve spring.
15. Ream new valve guides to the size given in DATA, then recut the valve seats and grind in the valves.
16. Check the cylinder head face for flatness and, if necessary, reface the cylinder head without reducing its depth below the figure given in DATA.
    NOTE: The combustion chamber inserts (if fitted) must be faced level with the cylinder head.
17. If necessary, reface the valves to the angle given in DATA, removing the minimum of material.
18. If necessary, recut the valve seats in the cylinder head, using the following tools:
    NOTE: Adjustable valve seat cutters MS 204 (exhaust), MS 621 (inlet) and expandable pilot MS 150-8.5, together with basic handle set MS 76, can be used as alternatives to the following glazing, cutting and narrowing tools.
    a 18G 27   Handle
    b 18G 174 D Pilot.
    c 18G 174 A Glaze breaker for inlet seats.
    d 18G 174   Cutter for inlet seats.

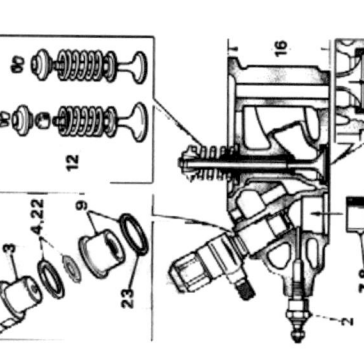
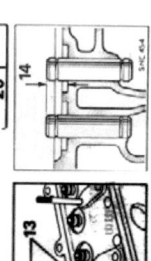

  e 18G 174 B Top narrowing cutter for inlet seats.
  f 18G 174 C Bottom narrowing cutter for inlet seats.
  g 18G 167 A Glaze breaker for exhaust seats.
  h 18G 167   Cutter for exhaust seats.
  j 18G 167 B Top narrowing cutter for exhaust seats.
  k 18G 167 C Bottom narrowing cutter for exhaust seats.
19. Lap the valves onto their seats, using tool 18G 29.
20. Check that the valve stand-down is within the limits given in DATA.
21. Renew the valve springs if they are not as specified in DATA.
22. Renew the sealing washers for the injectors.
23. Renew the sealing washers for the injector heat shields.
24. Reverse the procedure in 1 to 12.

DATA

Cylinder head
Depth after refacing .... 3.16 in (80.26 mm) minimum

Valve guides
Inside diameter (reamed after fitting) .. 0.3441 to 0.3448 in (8.74 to 8.76 mm)
Protrusion (from bottom of counterbore) .... 0.550 to 0.560 in (13.97 to 14.22 mm)

Valves
Seat angle .... 45°
Stand down: Inlet .... 0.0445 to 0.0505 in (1.13 to 1.28 mm)
            Exhaust .... 0.02 to 0.03 in (0.508 to 0.762 mm)
Stem diameter: Inlet .... 0.3428 to 0.3422 in (8.71 to 8.73 mm)
               Exhaust .... 0.3422 to 0.3427 in (8.69 to 8.70 mm)

Valve springs
Free length (approximate) .... 1 蓥 in (48.75 mm)
Load when compressed to 1.44 in (36.58 mm) .... 82 lbf, 37.20 kgf, 364 N

* 🔳 ***** 🔳 see page 7

VALVE CLEARANCE

Check and adjust   12.29.48

Checking
1. Remove the rocker cover and gasket.
2. Check, and if necessary adjust, the clearance between the rocker arms and valve stems against the figure in DATA, working in the following order:

Check:
No. 1 valve with No. 8 valve fully open.

```
"  3   "   "    "  6  "   "    "
"  5   "   "    "  4  "   "    "
"  2   "   "    "  7  "   "    "
"  8   "   "    "  1  "   "    "
"  6   "   "    "  3  "   "    "
"  4   "   "    "  5  "   "    "
"  7   "   "    "  2  "   "    "
```

Adjusting
3. Slacken the locknut.
4. Rotate the adjusting screw to set the clearance.
5. Hold the adjusting screw against rotation and tighten the locknut.
6. Fit the rocker cover and gasket.

DATA
Valve rocker clearance (cold) [1] **   0.017 in (0.43 mm)
                              [2] ..   0.014 in (0.36 mm)

** [1] [2] see page 7

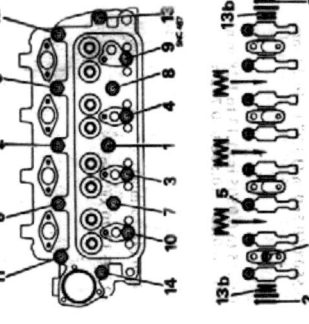

ROCKER SHAFT ASSEMBLY

Remove and refit   12.29.54
Service tool: 18G 694

Removing
1. Disconnect the battery.
2. Drain the cooling system.
3. Remove the rocker cover and gasket.
4. Slacken evenly and remove the eight nuts retaining the rocker shaft brackets.
5. Remove the locking plate from the rocker shaft rear bracket.
6. Remove the rocker shaft assembly and the shim under each centre bracket.

Refitting
7. Reverse the procedure in 1 to 6, noting:
   a. Tighten the cylinder head nuts to 75 lbf ft (10.4 kgf m, 102 Nm) in the sequence shown, using tool 18G 694 to reach the centre row. Tighten the rocker bracket nuts to 25 lbf ft (3.5 kgf m, 34 Nm).
   b. Adjust the valve rocker clearance, see 12.29.48.
8. Run the engine for a minimum of 5 miles, 8 km or 15 mins and on return slacken the cylinder head nuts approximately ¼ of a turn in the sequence shown before retightening them to 75 lbf ft (10.4 kgf m, 102 Nm) in the sequence shown. Check the valve rocker clearances.

ROCKER SHAFT ASSEMBLY

Overhaul   12.29.55
Service tools: 18G 226, 18G 226 A

Dismantling
1. Remove the rocker shaft, see 12.29.54.
2. Remove the split pin from each end of the rocker shaft.
3. Slide the components off the shaft.
4. Remove the locating screw from the rocker shaft rear bracket and remove the bracket.
5. Remove the adjuster screws.

Inspection
6. Clean the oilways of the rocker shaft.
7. Examine the rocker to valve contact faces for wear, and renew the rocker(s) if necessary.
8. Renew the rocker adjusting screws if they are worn or if the threads are damaged.
9. Press out worn rocker bushes, using tools 18G 226 and 18G 226 A.

Reassembling
10. Press in new rocker bushes, using tools 18G 226 and 18G 226 A, and ensuring that the bush joint and oil groove are in the positions shown.

11. Drill a hole in the bush, through the hole in the top of the rocker barrel, using a 1.95 mm drill.
12. Burnish-ream the bush to the dimension given in DATA.
13. Reverse the procedure in 1 to 5, noting:
    a. The locating screw engages the larger of the two diametrically opposite holes.
    b. The double-coil spring washers are fitted inside the plain washer at each end of the shaft.

DATA
Rocker shaft diameter ....   0.624 to 0.625 in (15.85 to 15.87 mm)
Rocker bush inside diameter (reamed in position) ....   0.6255 to 0.6260 in (15.89 to 15.90 mm)

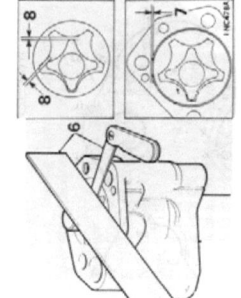

OIL PUMP

Overhaul 12.60.32

Dismantling
1. Remove the oil pump, see 12.10.30.
2. Remove the cover from the pump body.
   NOTE: The cover is located by two dowels.
3. Remove the rotors from the pump body.

Inspection
4. Clean the components.
5. Fit the rotors to the pump body with the chamfered end of the outer rotor at the closed end of the body.
6. Check the end-float of the inner and outer rotors.
7. Check the outer rotor to pump body diametrical clearance.
8. Check the rotor lobe clearances.
9. Renew the pump assembly if the clearances or end-floats in 6 to 8 exceed the figure given in DATA.

Reassembling
10. Lubricate all components with clean engine oil.
11. Reverse the procedure in 1 to 3, ensuring that the outer rotor is fitted with its chamfer at the closed end of the body.

DATA
Outer rotor end-float .... 0.005 in (0.13 mm)
Inner rotor end-float .... 0.005 in (0.13 mm)
Outer rotor to pump body diametrical
   clearance .... 0.010 in (0.25 mm)
Rotor lobe clearance .... 0.006 in (0.15 mm)

GOVERNED SPEEDS

Check and adjust 12.49.12

1. Run the engine until it reaches its normal operating temperature.
2. Fully open the butterfly.
3. Remove the seal. Slacken the locknut and unscrew the anti-stall screw on the injection pump three full turns.
4. Check the maximum speed and, if necessary, remove the sealing plug adjust the stop screw to set the correct maximum speed, see 'ENGINE TUNING DATA'.
5. Check the idling speed and, if necessary, adjust the stop screw to set the idling speed, see 'ENGINE TUNING DATA'.
   NOTE: Ensure that the injection pump throttle lever travel is not restricted by the control cable. If cable adjustment is necessary, adjust the cable which is connected to the injection pump.
6. Screw in the anti-stall screw until the idling speed is just affected then screw out the anti-stall screw two flats.
7. Tighten the locknut.
8. Close the butterfly.
9. Check that the injection pump throttle lever is operated through its complete range of movement by the throttle pedal, if necessary adjust the cable connected to the injection pump.
10. Start the engine and allow it to idle.
11. If there is excessive smoke from the exhaust with the engine idling, manually lift the butterfly control cam:
    a. If the exhaust smoke is reduced, adjust the butterfly.
    b. If lifting the cam does not reduce the smoke, check the fuel injection equipment.
12. Re-seal the maximum speed screw and the anti-stall screw.

OIL PRESSURE RELIEF VALVE

Remove and refit 12.60.56

Service tool: 18G 69

Removing

1 Disconnect the battery.
2 Remove the valve cap washer from the rear of the L.H. side of the crankcase.
3 Withdraw the spring from the crankcase.
4 Withdraw the valve plunger, using tool 18G 69.

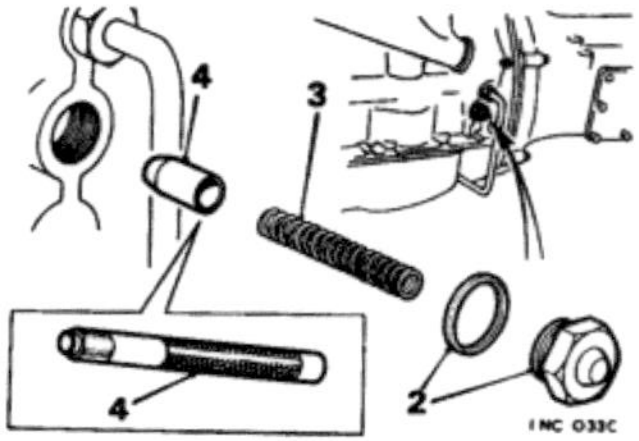

Refitting

5 If the valve plunger is pitted, or is not seating correctly, lap the plunger onto its seating, using tool 18G 69. If lapping fails to correct the fault, renew the plunger and ensure that the new plunger seats correctly.
6 Renew the spring if it is not as specified in DATA.
7 Reverse the procedure in 1 to 4.

DATA

Relief valve spring:

Free length	3 in (76 mm)
Load when compressed to 2.16 in (54.77 mm)	15.5 to 16.5 lbf (7.0 to 7.4 kgf, 69 to 73 N)

TIMING GEAR COVER OIL SEAL

Remove and refit 12.65.05

Timing gear cover – remove and refit 12.65.01

Service tools: 18G 98 A, 18G 134, 18G 134 BD

Removing

1 Disconnect the battery.
2 Slacken the alternator mounting bolts and remove the fan belt.
3 Remove the fan and water pump pulley.
4 Remove the crankshaft pulley, using tool 18G 98 A.
5 Remove the timing gear cover and gasket.
6 Remove the oil seal from the timing cover.

Refitting

7 Fit the new oil seal to the timing gear cover, using tools 18G 134 and 18G 134 BD.
8 Fit the timing gear cover and gasket, using the crankshaft pulley to centralize the oil seal on the crankshaft.
9 Fit the timing gear cover bolts in the following illustrated positions.

Position **Bolt size**
A 5/16 in x 1¾ in (44.5 mm) long
B 5/16 in x 2 in (50 mm) long
NOTE: An 'O' ring is fitted on this bolt.
C 5/16 in x 2 in (50 mm) long
D 5/16 in x 2¼ in (57 mm) long
E ¼ in x 1¾ in (44.5 mm) long
F ¼ in x 1¼ in (31.75 mm) long

0 Reverse the procedure in 1 to 4, tightening the crankshaft pulley bolt to 163 Nm (120 lbf ft, 16.6 kgf m) discarding the lock washer if fitted.

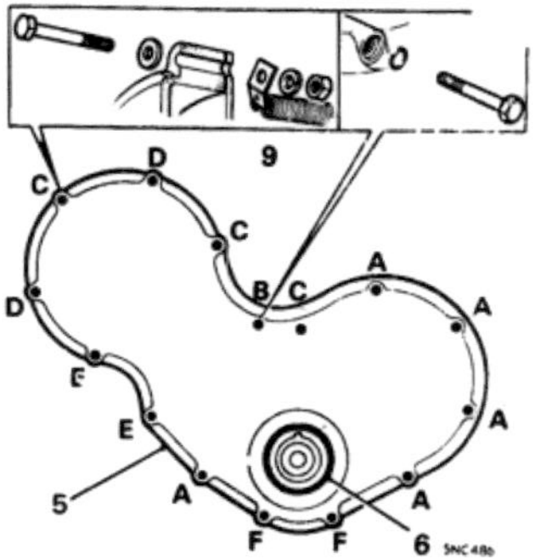

TIMING CHAIN AND GEARS

Remove and refit 12.65.12

Timing chain tensioner 1 to 14, 16 to 19, 34 to 40, and 43 to 47 12.65.28

Timing chain 1 to 14, 16 to 22, 29 to 41, and 43 to 47 12.65.14

Service tools: 18G 98 A, 18G 134, 18G 134 BD

Removing

1 Disconnect the battery.
2 Drain the cooling system.
3 Slacken the alternator mounting bolts and remove the fan belt.
4 Remove the fan and water pump pulley.
5 Remove the crankshaft pulley, using tool 18G 98 A.
6 Remove the timing gear cover and gasket.
7 Remove the crankshaft oil thrower.
8 If the camshaft gear is to be removed, slacken the camshaft nut using tool 18G 98 A.
9 Rotate the crankshaft until the timing marks are positioned as shown.
10 Hold the chain tensioner and chain together by hand and remove the tensioner retainer screw.
11 Lift away the chain tensioner.

12 If the chain tensioner shoe is to be renewed, remove the circlip from the pivot pin and lift off the shoe.
13 Remove the idler gear bolt.
14 Lift away the idler gear and its hub.
NOTE: The idler gear hub is located by a roll-pin dowel.
15 Remove the timing chain.
16 Remove the camshaft nut and gear.
17 Remove the crankshaft gear.

Refitting
18 Fit the camshaft gear and secure it with its nut.
19 Check the camshaft end-float against the figure in DATA. If end-float is excessive, remove the camshaft gear and renew the camshaft locating plate.
20 Fit the camshaft gear and crankshaft gear to their shafts.
21 Place a straight-edge across the tooth face of the gears and check their alignment; the crankshaft gear face should be rearward by the amount stated in DATA. If necessary, add or remove shims behind the crankshaft gear to set the alignment as near as possible to the DATA figure.
22 Position the injection pump gear with its timing hole at approximately 7 o'clock and insert a $\frac{7}{32}$ in (5.5 mm) peg through the hole to engage the hole in the engine front plate.
23 Position the camshaft gear and crankshaft gear with their timing marks in the positions shown.
24 Fit the timing chain and place the idler gear (without its hub) in position on the chain.
25 Adjust the position of the chain, without rotating the gears, to permit the idler gear hub to be fitted without chain slack between the idler and its adjacent gears.
NOTE: The idler gear hub is located by a roll-pin dowel.
26 Fit the idler gear bolt and tighten it to 30 lbf ft (4.1 kgf m, 41 Nm).
27 Fit the chain tensioner shoe and circlip to the pivot pin.
28 Fit the spring, pressure block, and centre pin to the chain tensioner body. Compress the spring and rotate the centre pin 180° to retain the compressed position.
29 Fit the pressure lever to the chain tensioner with the lever legs forward of the tensioner body, i.e. the tensioner body will contact the engine front plate when fitted.
30 Fit the retaining screw through the pressure lever and tensioner body.
31 Fit the compressed chain tensioner and tighten its retaining screw.
32 Rotate the centre pin 180° to release the tensioner.
33 Ensure that the timing marks are still correctly positioned.
34 Remove the peg from the injection pump gear.
35 Tighten the camshaft nut to 65 lbf ft (9 kgf m, 88 Nm).
36 Fit the crankshaft oil thrower with its dished side towards the gear.
37 Renew the timing gear cover oil seal, using tool 18G 134 and 18G 134 BD.
38 Fit the timing gear cover and gasket, using the crankshaft pulley to centralize the oil seal on the crankshaft.
39 Fit the timing cover bolts in the following illustrated positions.

Position	Bolt size
A	$\frac{5}{16}$ in x 1$\frac{3}{4}$ in (44.5 mm) long
B	$\frac{5}{16}$ in x 2 in (50 mm) long

NOTE: An 'O' ring is fitted on this bolt.
C	$\frac{3}{8}$ in x 2 in (50 mm) long
D	$\frac{3}{8}$ in x 2$\frac{1}{4}$ in (57 mm) long
E	$\frac{3}{8}$ in x 1$\frac{3}{4}$ in (44.5 mm) long
F	$\frac{3}{8}$ in x 1$\frac{1}{4}$ in (31.75 mm) long

40 Reverse the procedure in 1 to 5, tightening the crankshaft pulley bolt to 156 Nm, 115 lbf ft, 16 kgf m discarding the lockwasher if fitted.

DATA
Camshaft end-float .. 0.003 to 0.007 in (0.08 to 0.18 mm)
Timing gear alignment .. Crankshaft gear 0.000 to 0.005 in (0.00 mm to 0.13 mm) rearward of camshaft gear.

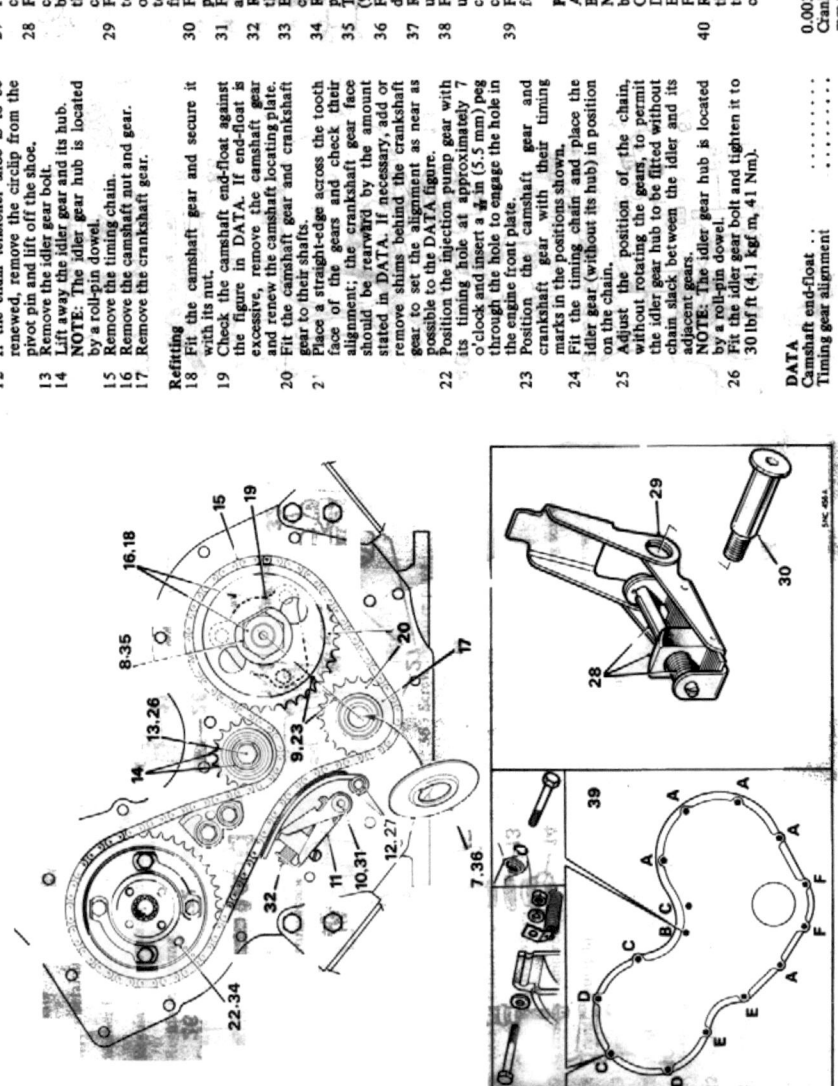

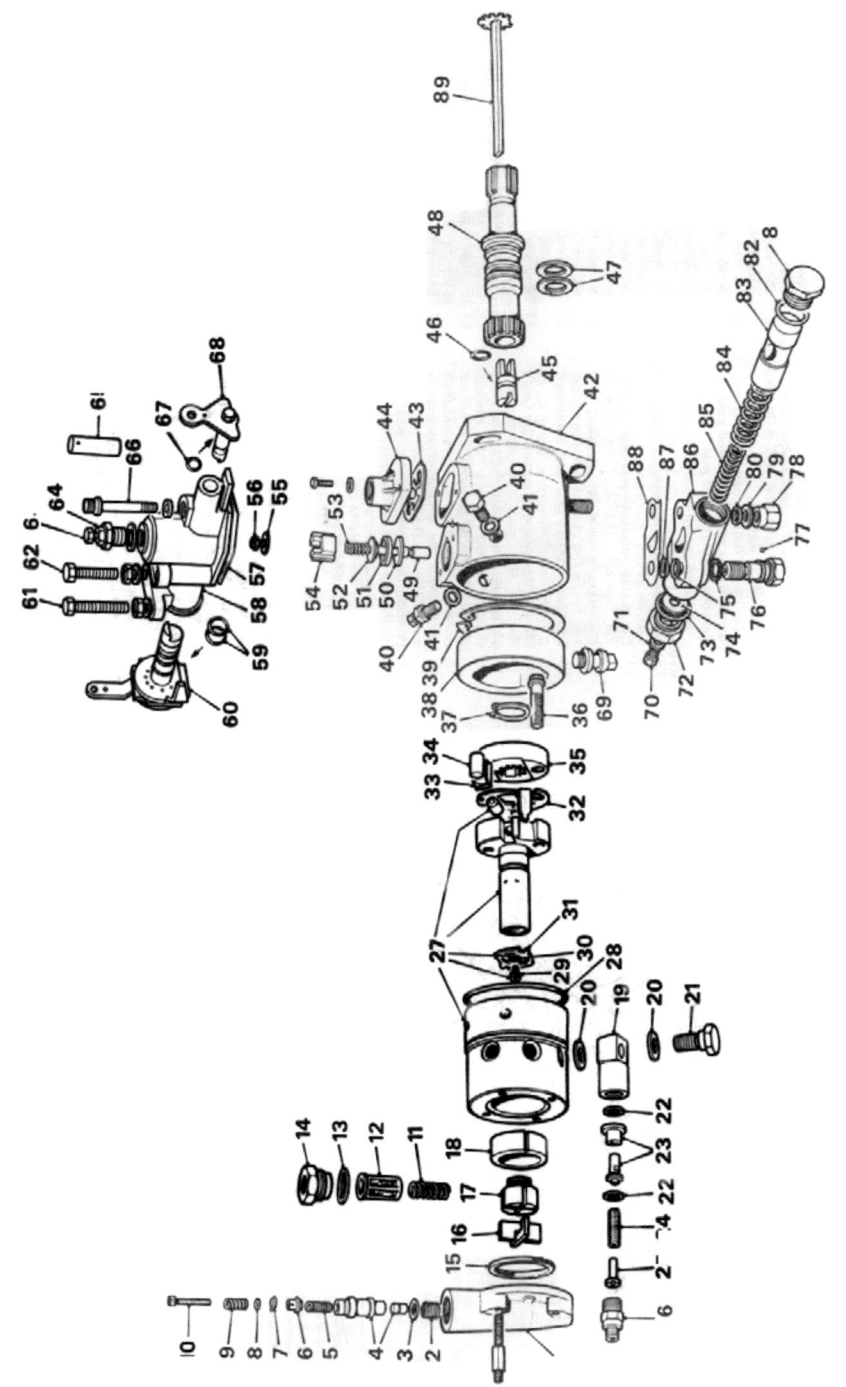

KEY TO THE HYDRAULIC GOVERNOR INJECTION PUMP COMPONENTS

1. End plate
2. Piston retaining spring
3. Washer for sleeve
4. Regulating sleeve and piston
5. Regulating spring
6. Guide plug for sleeve
7. Torsion spring
8. Washer for plug
9. Spring for adjusting screw
10. Adjusting screw
11. Sleeve retaining spring
12. Filter
13. Washer for inlet connection
14. Fuel inlet connection
15. Seal for transfer pump
16. Transfer pump vanes
17. Transfer pump rotor
18. Transfer pump liner
19. Banjo
20. Washer for banjo bolt
21. Banjo bolt
22. Washer for delivery valve seat
23. Delivery valve and seat
24. Delivery valve spring
25. Spring guide
26. Delivery valve holder
27. Hydraulic head and rotor assembly
28. Seal for hydraulic head
29. End plug for rotor
30. Washer for plug
31. Bottom adjusting plate
32. Top adjusting plate
33. Shoe for roller
34. Roller
35. Drive plate
36. Screw for drive plate
37. Circlip for drive shaft
38. Cam ring
39. Circlip for cam ring
40. Hydraulic head locking screw
41. Washer for locking screw
42. Pump body
43. Gasket for cover
44. Adjusting hole cover
45. Guide dog
46. 'O' ring
47. Seals for drive shaft
48. Drive shaft
49. Metering valve
50. Damping valve seating washer
51. Damping valve centre washer
52. Damping valve spring plate
53. Governor spring
54. Control sleeve
55. Shut-off washer
56. Nut for metering valve
57. Gasket for governor housing
58. Governor housing
59. 'O' rings
60. Throttle shaft
61. Idling speed stop screw
62. Maximum speed stop screw
63. Bleed screw
64. Anti-stall screw
65. Locking sleeve
66. Screw for governor housing
67. 'O' ring
68. Shut-off shaft
69. Cam advance screw
70. Screw for spring cap
71. Washer for screw
72. Spring cap
73. 'O' ring
74. Shim(s)
75. 'O' ring
76. Head locating bolt
77. Non-return valve ball
78. Cap nut
79. Washer for cap nut
80. Seal for cap nut
81. End plug
82. 'O' ring
83. Advance piston
84. Outer spring for piston
85. Inner spring for piston
86. Advance housing
87. Washer for head locating bolt
88. Gasket
89. Torsion bar

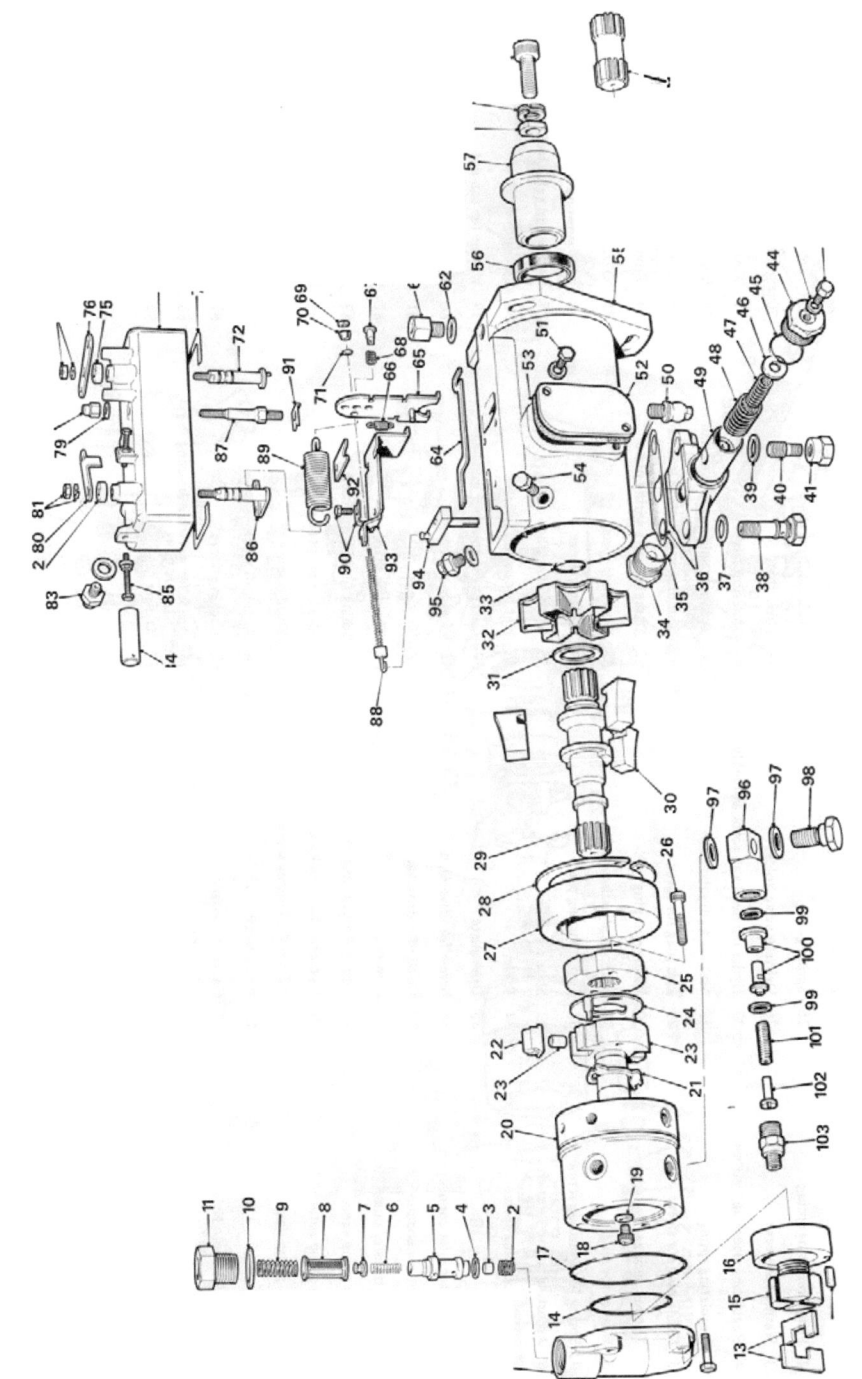

KEY TO THE MECHANICAL GOVERNOR INJECTION PUMP COMPONENTS

1. End plate
2. Priming spring
3. Regulating piston
4. Washer for sleeve
5. Regulating sleeve
6. Regulating spring
7. End plate sleeve plug
8. Filter
9. Sleeve retaining spring
10. Inlet connection washer
11. Fuel inlet connection
12. Locating pin
13. Transfer pump vanes
14. Transfer pump seal
15. Transfer pump rotor
16. Transfer pump liner
17. Hydraulic head seal
18. Rotor plug
19. Washer for plug
20. Hydraulic head
21. Bottom adjusting plate
22. Roller shoe
23. Roller
24. Top adjusting plate
25. Drive plate
26. Drive plate screw
27. Cam ring
28. Cam ring locating circlip
29. Drive shaft
30. Governor weight
31. Thrust washer
32. Governor weights retainer
33. Drive shaft seal
34. Plug
35. Plug seal
36. Automatic advance device housing and gasket
37. Head locating bolt washer
38. Head locating bolt
39. Cap nut washer
40. Stud
41. Stud cap nut
42. Cap screw
43. Screw seal
44. Cap piston spring
45. Cap seal
46. Spring shim
47. Piston inner spring
48. Piston outer spring
49. Piston
50. Cam advance screw
51. Cover plate screw
52. Cover plate
53. Cover plate gasket
54. Bleed screw
55. Pump housing
56. Drive hub seal
57. Drive hub
58. Support washer
59. Screw spring washer
60. Drive shaft screw
61. Drive shaft
62. Connection washer
63. Drain connection
64. Shut-off bar
65. Governor arm
66. Governor arm spring
67. Idling spring guide
68. Idling spring
69. Linkage nut
70. Pivot ball washer
71. Linkage washer
72. Shut-off shaft
73. Control cover gasket
74. Control cover
75. Dust cap
76. Shut-off lever
77. Nut and washer
78. Nut
79. Washer
80. Throttle arm
81. Nut and washer
82. Dust cap
83. Bleed screw
84. Locking sleeve
85. Adjusting screw
86. Throttle shaft
87. Stud
88. Linkage hook and spring
89. Governor spring
90. Screw and tab washer
91. Tab washer
92. Keep plate
93. Control bracket
94. Metering valve
95. Bleed screw
96. Banjo
97. Washer for banjo bolt
98. Banjo bolt
99. Washer for delivery valve seat
100. Delivery valve and seat
101. Delivery valve spring
102. Spring guide
103. Delivery valve holder

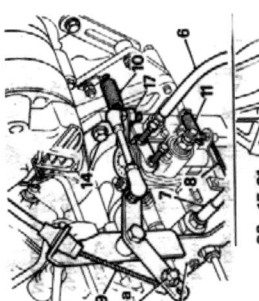  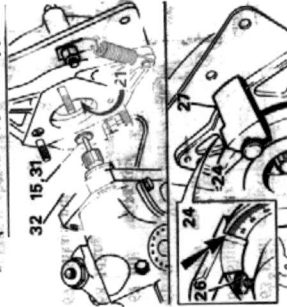 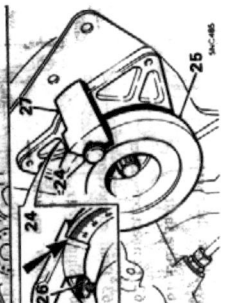

25 Insert the assembled tool into the injection pump position on the engine, engaging the injection pump drive splines.
26 Slide the body of the tool along its centre bar until the body engages the injection pump drive gear hub. Lock the centre bar with the knurled screw.
27 Apply gentle pressure to the tool and (the rear) check that the scribed line (timing mark) on the drive gear hub lines up with the scribing guide of the tool. If necessary, scribe a new mark.
28 Remove tool MS 67A.
29 Remove timing pin AMK 9990.
30 Fit the injection pump gasket to the drive gear hub.
31 Hydraulically governed pumps: Fit the torsion bar into the drive flange on the engine.
32 Position the injection pump drive shaft so that its master spline lines up with that on the drive flange.
33 Fit the injection pump drive shaft over the end of the torsion bar and VERY GENTLY engage the drive shaft splines with the drive flange splines.
34 Push the injection pump as far into position as possible and fit the spring anchor bracket, washers, and nuts.
35 Progressively tighten the three nuts to pull the injection pump fully into position, ensuring that the timing marks on the pump and drive flange are aligned.
36 Reverse the procedure in 1 to 13, noting:
 a Ensure that the throttle cable is connected to the inner hole in the bell crank lever, and that the injection pump throttle lever is operated through its full range of movement by the throttle pedal.
 b After the stop control cable is connected, ensure that the stop control has sufficient travel to permit removal of the master/starter switch key.
37 Bleed the fuel system, see 19.50.07.
38 Adjust the engine maximum and idling speeds, see 12.49.12.

23 Maintain a light pressure on the timing pin and rotate the crankshaft in the normal direction of rotation until the timing pin engages the timing hole in the flywheel. The master spline in the injection pump drive should now be in the 8 o'clock position when viewed from the rear.
24 Assemble the long scribing guide of tool MS 67A to the tool body, set it on the $204°$ position (hydraulically governed pumps) or $205°$ position (mechanically governed pumps), and lock it with its knurled screw.

Removing
1 Disconnect the battery.
2 Slacken the alternator mounting bolts and remove the fan belt.
3 Remove the alternator.
4 Disconnect the lead from the thermal transmitter.
5 Disconnect the supply lead from the heater plugs.
6 Disconnect the fuel return pipe from the injection pump.
7 Disconnect the fuel supply pipe from the injection pump.
8 Disconnect the stop control cable from the injection pump.
9 Disconnect the throttle cable from the injection pump bracket and bell crank lever.
10 Remove the injection pump throttle lever return spring.
11 Remove the injection pump stop lever return spring.
12 Remove Nos. 3 and 4 injector pipes.
13 Remove Nos. 1 and 2 injector pipes.
14 Remove the three nuts and washers securing the injection pump and withdraw the injection pump from the engine.
NOTE: The lower nut also secures the anchor bracket for the stop lever return spring.
15 Withdraw the injection pump torsion bar.
16 Remove the injection pump gasket.
17 Disconnect the control plate linkage from the throttle lever on the injection pump.
18 Remove the control plate assembly from the injection pump.

Refitting
19 Fit the control plate assembly to the injection pump.
20 Connect the control plate linkage to the throttle lever on the injection pump.
21 Rotate the crankshaft until the master spline in the injection pump drive is in the 12 o'clock position.
22 Insert timing pin AMK 9990 into the timing hole in the gearbox adaptor plate. The hole is situated below the sump flange on the RH side.

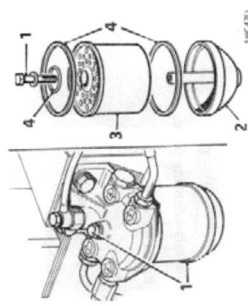

FUEL FILTER ELEMENT 19.25.07

Remove and refit

Removing
1 Support the filter base and unscrew the centre bolt in the filter head.
2 Detach the filter base.
3 Remove the element, using a twisting motion.
4 Remove the seals from the filter base and filter head.

Refitting
5 Clean the filter base.
6 Reverse the procedure in 1 to 4, using a new element and seals.
7 Bleed the fuel system, see 19.50.07.

INJECTION PUMP

Remove and refit 19.30.07
Timing — check and adjust 19.30.01
1 to 16 and 21 to 38

Service tools: AMK 9990, MS 67 A

NOTE: The illustration shows a hydraulically governed pump, but some engines are fitted with a mechanically governed pump which will not be fitted with a torsion bar.

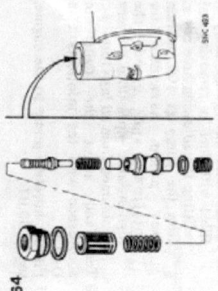

50

55

64

INJECTION PUMP (Hydraulically Governed)

Overhaul 19.30.19

Service tools: 18G 109 A, 18G 634, 18G 635, 18G 633 A, 18G 637, 18G 638 B, 18G 636, 18G 640, 18G 641, 18G 639, 18G 646, 18G 643 A, 18G 651, 18G 653 A, 18G 648 A, 18G 656, 18G 690, 18G 655 A, 18G 1004, 18G 691 A,

Dismantling

1. Remove the injection pump, see 19.30.07.
2. Mount the pump on assembly base 18G 633 A.

NOTE: Immerse components in clean calibration fluid as the pump is dismantled.

3. Remove the delivery valves from the high pressure connections, keeping each delivery valve with its own seat.
4. Remove the high-pressure connections.
5. Remove the adjusting hole cover.
6. Remove the governor housing and withdraw the securing screws from it.
7. Withdraw the throttle shaft.
8. Withdraw the shut-off shaft.
9. Withdraw the metering valve assembly.
10. Dismantle the metering valve assembly, using tool 18G 637.
11. Remove the advance unit, noting the non-return valve ball in the side of the hydraulic head locating bolt.
12. Remove the spring cap from the advance unit, noting the shim(s) inside the spring cap.
13. Lift out the advance unit springs.
14. Remove the end plug from the advance unit.
15. Remove the piston from the advance unit.
16. Remove the cam ring advance screw, using tool 18G 646.
17. Slacken the inlet connection.
18. Withdraw the transfer pump vanes.
19. Withdraw the transfer pump liner.
20. Remove the fuel inlet connection from the end plate.
21. Withdraw the regulating valve components.
22.
23. Slacken the transfer pump rotor, using tools 18G 634 and 18G 651.
24. Remove both locking screws and withdraw the hydraulic head assembly.
25. Unscrew the transfer pump rotor.
26. Remove the drive plate, using tool 18G 641.
27. Lift off the top adjusting plate.
28. Remove the rollers and shoes.
29. Withdraw the rotor.
30. Remove the bottom adjusting plate.
31. Withdraw the cam ring from the pump body.
32. Withdraw the cam ring circlip, using tool 18G 1004.
33. Remove the drive shaft circlip, using tool 18G 1004.
34. Withdraw the drive shaft from the pilot tube.
35. Remove the guide dog from the inner end of the drive shaft.

Inspection

36. Renew all 'O' rings, oil seals, and gaskets.
37. Renew any springs which are damaged or of incorrect length when compared with new counterparts.
38. Examine the hydraulic head, rotor, pumping plungers, and metering valve. If any of these components are worn or damaged, renew the hydraulic head and rotor assembly.
39. Renew the cam ring and plunger rollers if they show signs of wear or flats.
40. Renew the regulating valve sleeve and piston if they are worn or if the piston is tight in the sleeve.
41. Renew the pump body if the pilot tube bore is scored or worn.

Reassembling

42. Fit the drive shaft seals, using tool 18G 635.
NOTE: Ensure that the seals settle with their concave sides towards the pump end of the drive shaft.
43. Fit the 'O' ring to the guide dog.
44. Fit the guide dog into the drive shaft.
45. Fit the drive shaft to the pump body, rotating the shaft continually and allowing the assembly of shaft and seals to enter the pilot tube under its own weight.
46. Fit the drive shaft circlip, using tool 18G 1004.
47. Fit the cam ring circlip to the pump body, using tool 18G 1004.
48. Fit the cam ring, ensuring that the directional arrow on its visible face matches the direction of the arrow on the pump nameplate.
49. Fit the cam ring advance screw finger tight.
50. Fit the top adjusting plate and the drive plate as shown, leaving the screws finger tight.
51. Fit the roller and shoe assemblies.
52. Fit the bottom adjusting plate.
53. Insert the rotor assembly into the hydraulic head.
54. Fit the transfer pump rotor finger tight.
55. Set the roller-to-roller dimension at the figure given in DATA, using tools 18G 653 A (preset at 15 Atm) and 18G 109 A.
56. Tighten the drive plate screws to 140 lbf in (1,61 kgf m, 15 Nm), using tools 18G 641 and 18G 655 A.
57. Fit the 'O' ring to the hydraulic head periphery.
58. Fit the hydraulic head to the pump body.
NOTE: In addition to aligning the master spline of the drive plate and drive shaft, it is necessary to align the slot in the guide dog with the rotor.
59. Fit both hydraulic head locking screws finger tight.
NOTE: The locking screw incorporating a bleed screw is fitted next to the pump nameplate.
60. Tighten the transfer pump rotor to 65 lbf in (0,75 kgf m, 7,4 Nm) using tools 18G 634 and 18G 651.
61. Fit the transfer pump liner.
62. Fit the transfer pump vanes.
63. Ensure that the transfer pump liner locating pin is fitted to position 'C' in the end plate.
64. Assemble the regulating valve components to the end plate in the order shown.
65. Locate the oil sealing ring on the hydraulic head face and fit the end plate.
66. Tighten the end plate studs to 45 lbf in (0,52 kgf m, 4 Nm).

continued

67 Tighten the fuel inlet connection to 450 lbf in (5.18 kgf m, 50 Nm).
68 Tighten the cam ring advance screw to 450 lbf in (5.18 kgf m, 50 Nm) using tool 18G 646. Ensure that the cam ring is free.
69 Fit the 'O' rings to the advance unit end plug and spring cap, using tool 18G 640.
70 Fit the end plug to the advance unit at the end where the fuel drilling enters the bore.
71 Fit the piston, closed end leading, into the advance unit.
72 Fit the spring cap, with its original thickness of shim(s), to the advance unit.
73 Fit the springs into the piston.
74 Fit the 'O' ring to the hydraulic head locating bolt, using tool 18G 639.
75 Fit the non-return valve ball to its seat in the side of the head locating bolt and fit the bolt to the advance unit.
76 Fit the 'O' ring to the shank of the head locating bolt, using tool 18G 647, and fit the plain washer on top of the 'O' ring.
77 Fit the advance unit and its gasket leaving the head locating bolt finger tight.
78 Fit the advance unit cap nut and washer finger tight.
79 Assemble the metering valve components in the order shown, using tool 18G 637 when tightening the nut.
80 Fit the 'O' rings to the throttle shaft, using tool 18G 643 A.
81 Fit the 'O' ring to the shut off shaft using tool 18G 647.
82 Unscrew the idling stop screw.
83 Insert the metering valve assembly into the governor housing and fit the throttle shaft with its end engaging between the shut-off washer and the control sleeve.
84 Fit the shut-off shaft to the governor housing and ensure that both control shafts operate the metering valve correctly.
85 Use tool 18G 691 A to accurately align the metering valve bore in the hydraulic head with the damping valve bore in the pump body, then tighten both hydraulic head locking screws to

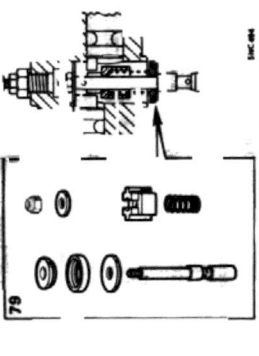

170 lbf in (1.95 kgf m, 18 Nm). Ensure that tool 18G 691 A is still completely free to rotate.
86 Tighten the advance unit cap nut to 130 lbf in (1.5 kgf m, 14 Nm).
87 Tighten the hydraulic head locating bolt to 350 lbf in (4.05 kgf m, 39 Nm).
88 Tighten the advance unit end plug and spring cap to 250 lbf in (2.9 kgf m, 28 Nm).
89 Fit the governor housing and joint washer.
NOTE: The throttle lever should be on the nameplate side of the pump.
90 Fit the adjusting hole cover and gasket.
91 Fit the high-pressure connections.
NOTE: The connection with the bleed screw is fitted to outlet 'X'.
92 Fit the delivery valves to the high-pressure connections.
93 Mount the pump on a test bench.
94 Remove the plain hydraulic head locking screw and fit adaptor 18G 636.
95 Fit end plate adjuster 18G 690 to the inlet connection. Unscrew the adjuster fully then screw it in 1½ turns.
96 Remove the screw from the advance unit spring cap and fit advance gauge 18G 638 B. Zero the gauge.
97 Set the stop screws to give maximum throttle lever movement.
98 Make the following pump to test bench connections:
  a Delivery valves to injectors.
  b Hydraulic head adaptor to pressure gauge.

99 End plate adjuster to feed pipe (with a branch off to vacuum gauge).
  Adjusting hole cover, via measuring glass, to drain pipe.
  Prime the injection pump as follows:
  a Turn on the fuel feed.
  b Slacken the feed pipe at the injection pump until the fuel flowing from it is free of air bubbles then tighten the feed pipe.
  c Air vent the pump from the hydraulic head bleed screw.
  d Rotate the pump drive through 90° and again vent the hydraulic head.
  e Air vent the pump from the bleed screw on the governor housing.
  f Check that the pump body is filled with fuel by removing and refitting the adjusting hole cover.
  g Run the pump at 100 rev/min (see pump nameplate for rotation) and bleed the high-pressure pipes until delivery is obtained from all injectors.
100 Test and adjust the pump in accordance with the information in DATA.
101 Fit the injection pump to the engine, see 19.30.07.

DATA
Roller to roller dimension:
DPA.3247F180 ...... 50.30 mm (1.980 in)
DPA.3247F260 ...... 50.14 mm (1.974 in)

Testing
Conditions of test:
1 The test bench must be set to run in the direction of pump rotation.
2 Fuel available at the pump inlet must be 1,000 cm³ per minute flow minimum, or 2 lbf/in² (0.15 kgf/cm²) pressure maximum.
3 Test injectors should be a matched set with type BDN.12.SD.12 nozzles operating at 175 Atm.
4 Injector pipes should be 6 mm x 2 mm x 34 in (865 mm) long.
5 The injection pump throttle and shut-off levers must be in the fully open position, except where stated otherwise.
6 All fuel delivery figures are for 200 shots.
7 Allow 30 seconds glass draining time and 15 seconds oil settling time when taking fuel delivery readings.
8 The maximum fuel delivery given in the 'Test plan' is for sea-level conditions. For continuous use above sea-level the maximum fuel delivery should be set as follows:

	Maximum fuel delivery	
Altitude	Code 32/1200/0/4900	Code 27E/1200/0/4900
0 to 2,000 ft (0 to 600 m)	6.2 to 6.4 cm³	5.2 to 5.4 cm³
2,000 to 4,000 ft (600 to 1200 m)	5.8 to 6.0 cm³	4.8 to 5.0 cm³
4,000 to 6,000 ft (1200 to 1800 m)	5.4 to 5.6 cm³	4.4 to 4.6 cm³
6,000 to 8,000 ft (1800 to 2400 m)	5.0 to 5.2 cm³	4.0 to 4.2 cm³
8,000 to 10,000 ft (2400 to 3000 m)	4.6 to 4.8 cm³	3.7 to 3.9 cm³
10,000 to 12,000 ft (3000 to 3600 m)	4.2 to 4.4 cm³	3.4 to 3.6 cm³

continued

Test plan for pumps with setting codes 27E/1200/0/4900 or 32/1200/0/4900
NOTE: The figures qualified * apply to either pump when using Hartridge test machines type 800, 875 and 1100. The figures qualified † apply to either pump when using any other test machine.

TEST No.	DESCRIPTION	REV/MIN	REQUIREMENTS	REMARKS
1	Transfer pump vacuum	100	16 in Hg (406 mm) within 60 seconds	Fuel supply turned off. Air vent from hydraulic head bleed screw at 100 rev/min after test
2	Transfer pressure	100	11 lbf/in² (0.8 kgf/cm²) minimum	If necessary, exchange the regulating sleeve guide plug to obtain this pressure
3	Transfer pressure	1,200	*39 to 51 lbf/in² (2.7 to 3.6 kgf/cm²) †38 to 50 lbf/in² (2.6 to 3.5 kgf/cm²)	Adjust as in Test 2 to obtain pressure
4	Transfer pressure	2,200	As Test 3 plus *36 lbf/in² (2.5 kgf/cm²) †34 lbf/in² (2.4 kgf/cm²)	Adjust by means of end plate adjuster 18G 69○○
5	Advance position	1,200	*3° to 3½° †2½° to 3°	Adjust by adding shims inside the advance unit spring cap to a maximum of 3.0 mm additional to the original 0.5 mm shim which must remain
6	Advance position	800	6¾° to 7¼°	
7	Back-leakage	,200	5 to 50 cm³ per 100 — shot time cycle	
8	Maximum fuel delivery	,200	*5.3 ± 0.1 cm³ (spread between lines) †6.4 +0.0 cm³ (not to exceed 0.5 cm³) See item 8 in 'Conditions of test'	Adjust output by moving adjusting plate relative to drive plate with tool 18G 656. Tighten the drive plate screws to 140 lbf in (1.61 kgf m, 15 Nm) with tool 18G 655 A
9	Fuel delivery	100	Average to be not less than average in Test 8 minus *2.2 cm³ †2.0 cm³	
10	Cut-off operation	200	Average 0.5 cm³ maximum	Shut-off lever fully closed
11	Fuel delivery	*2,000 †2,300	Record delivery	
12	Governor setting	*2,350 †2,700	Average 1.0 cm³ maximum (no line to exceed 1.5 cm³)	Set throttle lever with maximum speed adjustment screw
13	Fuel delivery	*2,000 †2,300	Average to be not less than average in Test 11 minus *0.4 cm³ †0.3 cm³	Throttle lever set as in 12
14	Transfer pressure	2,200	As Test 3 plus *36 lbf/in² (2.5 kgf/cm²) †34 lbf/in² (2.4 kgf/cm²)	First unscrew maximum speed adjustment screw, then adjust by means of end plate adjuster 18G 690
15	Governor setting	*2,350 †2,700	Average 1.0 cm³ maximum (no line to exceed 1.5 cm³)	Set throttle lever with maximum speed adjustment screw
16	Timing			Adaptor 18G 653 A (set at 30 Atm) connecting 18G 109 A to outlet 'Y'. Apply fuel pressure, rotate drive shaft tool 18G 648 A (set at 204°) and mark pump flange with scriber

Test plan for pumps with setting codes A21E/600/0/3480

NOTE: The figures apply to when using Hartridge test machines type 800, 875 and 100.

TEST No.	DESCRIPTION	REV/MIN	REQUIREMENTS	REMARKS
1	Priming	100 max.	Fuel delivery from all injectors	
2	Transfer pressure	100	10 lbf/in² (0.7 kgf/cm²) minimum	If necessary, exchange the regulating guide plug to obtain this pressure
3	Transfer pressure	1,100	36 to 46 lbf/in² (2.5 to 3.2 kgf/cm²)	Adjust as in Test 2 to obtain pressure
4	Advance position	1,100	3¾° to 3¾°	Adjust by adding shims inside the advance unit spring cap to a maximum of 3.0 mm additional to the original 0.5 mm shim which must remain
5	Advance check	1,800	With throttle lever closed, advance to be 6¾° to 7¾°	
6	Back leakage	1,100	5 to 50 cm³ per 100-stroke time cycle	
7	Maximum fuel delivery	600*	4.1 ± 0.1 cm³ (spread between lines not to exceed 0.5 cm³)	Adjust output by moving adjusting plate relative to drive plate with tool 18G 656. Tighten the drive plate screws to 140 lbf in (1.61 kgf m, 15 Nm) with tool 18G 655 A
8	Fuel delivery	100*	Average to be not less than average in Test 7	
9	Cut-off operation	200	Average 0.5 cm² maximum	Shut-off lever fully closed
10	Fuel delivery	1,500	Record delivery	
11	Governor setting	1,740	Average 1.0 cm³ maximum (no line to exceed 1.5 cm³)	Set throttle lever with maximum speed adjustment screw
12	Fuel delivery	1,500	Average to be not less than average in Test 10 minus 0.4 cm³	Throttle lever set as in 11
13	Timing			Adaptor 18G 653 A (set at 30 Atm.) connecting 18G 109 A to outlet 'V'. Apply fuel pressure, rotate drive shaft tool 18G 648 A (set at 204°) and mark pump flange with scriber

* Use 30 seconds glass draining time and allow fuel to settle for 15 seconds before taking reading.

LIFT PUMP

Removing 19.45.09
1. Disconnect the battery.
2. Disconnect the two pipes from the lift pump.
3. Plug the supply pipe from the fuel tank.
4. Remove the securing nuts and washers.
5. Remove the lift pump and gasket.

Refitting
6. Reverse the procedure in 1 to 5.
7. Bleed the fuel system, see 19.50.07.

LIFT PUMP

Overhaul 19.45.16

Dismantling
1. Remove the lift pump, see 19.45.09.
2. Scribe a reassembly mark across the body joint flanges.
3. Remove the domed cover and sealing ring.
4. Remove the filter.
5. Remove the securing screws and separate the top and bottom halves of the pump.
6. If the valves require renewing, lever them out carefully.
7. Remove the valve gaskets.
8. Press the diaphragm downwards, rotate it through 90° and withdraw it
9. Lift out the diaphragm spring.
10. If the diaphragm rod seal is to be renewed, carefully withdraw the seal retainer.
11. Lift out the seal.
12. If the rocker arm pin or linkage is to be renewed, secure the rocker arm in a vice and tap the face of the pump mounting flange to dislodge the rocker arm pin and its components.

Reassembling
13. Renew any components which are worn or damaged.
14. Reverse the procedure in 1 to 12, noting:
    a. If the diaphragm spring is renewed, ensure that the new spring is of the same colour as the original.

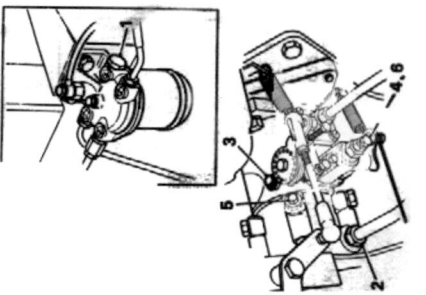

FUEL SYSTEM

Bleeding 19.50.07

WARNING: Do not attempt to bleed the system by towing the vehicle in gear as this would result in serious damage to the injection pump.

NOTE: After renewing the fuel filter element it will only be necessary to bleed the fuel filter as described in 1 and 2, provided that the engine has not been cranked while the filter is dismantled.

1. Slacken the blanking plug in the unused outlet connection in the fuel filter head. Operate the lift pump by means of its priming lever and, when the fuel flowing from the plug is free of air bubbles, tighten the plug.
2. Slacken the union nut at the injection pump end of the fuel feed pipe. Operate the lift pump and, when the fuel flowing from the union is free of air bubbles, tighten the nut.
3. Slacken the air bleed screw on the injection pump body. Operate the lift pump and, when the fuel flowing from the bleed screw is free of air bubbles, tighten the screw.
4. Slacken the air bleed screw on the injection pump governor housing. Operate the lift pump until the fuel flowing from the bleed screw is free of air bubbles, leave the bleed screw slack.
5. Slacken the air bleed screw on the injection pump high-pressure banjo bolt. Operate the starter motor while pressing the accelerator pedal down and, when the fuel flowing from the high-pressure bleed screw is free of air bubbles, tighten the bleed screw. Continue cranking the engine with the starter motor to expel any air trapped in the governor and, when the fuel flowing from the governor housing bleed screw is free of air bubbles, tighten the bleed screw.

b. If the valves are renewed, ensure that they are fitted to operate in the correct directions and staked in.

NOTE: The inlet port is indicated by an arrow on the pump body.

Slacken the union nut at the injector end of any two high-pressure pipes. Operate the starter motor while pressing the accelerator pedal down, and when the fuel flowing from both pipes is free of air bubbles, tighten both union nuts.
Start the engine and allow it to run until it is firing on all cylinders.

INJECTORS

Remove and refit 19.60.01

Service tools: 18G 284, 18G 284 P

Removing
1. Disconnect the battery.
2. Disconnect the spill rail from the injectors.
3. Disconnect the high-pressure pipes from the injectors.
4. Remove the nuts and washers securing the injectors.
5. Withdraw the injectors, using tools 18G 284 and 18G 284 P if necessary.
6. Remove the two sealing washers from each injector position.

Refitting
7. Fit two new sealing washers to each injector position, fitting the smaller washer as shown.
8. Reverse the procedure in 1 to 5, tightening the injector securing nuts to 12 lbf ft (1.7 kgf m, 16 Nm).
9. If more than two injectors have been removed, crank the engine with the starter motor and bleed at least two of the high-pressure pipes.

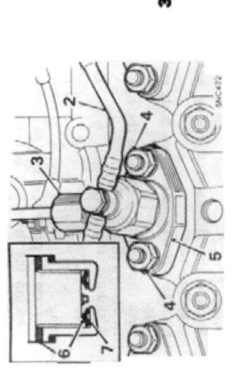

INJECTORS

Overhaul 19.60.08

Service tools: 18G 109 A, 18G 109 B, 18G 109 E, 18G 210, 18G 388, 18G 487

1. Remove the injectors, see 19.60.01.
2. Mount the injector in tool 18G 388.
3. Remove the cap nut and sealing washer.
4. Remove the spring cap and shim.
5. Remove the spring.
6. Lift out the spindle.
7. Remove the nozzle nut and nozzle, using tool 18G 210.
8. Renew the spring if it shows any sign of weakness or distortion.
9. Renew the spindle if it is not perfectly straight.
10. Clean the nozzle and valve, using kit 18G 487.
11. Reverse-flush the nozzle, using tools 18G 109 A and 18G 109 E.
12. Renew the nozzle assembly if the pintle clearance allows an angle of more than 20° when checked as shown.
13. If necessary, restore the nozzle and valve seats to the angles given in DATA.
14. Check the needle lift against the figure in DATA.
15. Reverse the procedure in 2 to 7, tightening the nozzle nut to 50 lbf ft (6.9 kgf m, 68 Nm).
16. Test and set the injectors to the specification given in DATA, using tools 18G 109 A and 18G 109 B.
17. Fit the injectors, see 19.60.01.

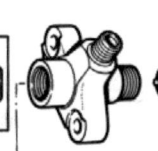

DATA
Auxiliary hole diameter .... 0.2 mm
Needle lift .... 0.70 to 0.75 mm
Nozzle seat angle .... 59° 0'
Valve seat angle .... 60° 0'

Testing

TEST		NOZZLE SET TO OPEN AT	ADAPTOR (18G 109 B) SET TO OPEN AT	STROKES PER MINUTE	REQUIREMENTS
Spray	Auxiliary	135 Atm	220 Atm	60	Spray free of distortions. Slight core permissible.
	Main	135 Atm	220 Atm	140	Spray free of distortions. Slight core permissible.
Seat tightness		100 Atm	–	–	Dry nozzle after 10 seconds at 90 Atm pressure
Back-leakage		160 to 170 Atm	–	–	Initial pressure 160 Atm. Time for pressure drop from 150 to 100 Atm to be between 6 and 140 seconds
Final setting		135 Atm*	–	–	

*Add 5 Atm when setting new injectors or after fitting new springs.

COOLANT

Drain and refill 26.10.01

Draining

WARNING: If the cooling system is hot, remove the filler cap slowly to release the pressure from the cooling system.
1. Remove the filler cap.
2. Slacken the clip and disconnect the bottom hose from the radiator.
3. Remove the cylinder block drain plug.

Refitting

4. Refit the cylinder block drain plug.
5. Reconnect the bottom hose to the radiator and tighten the clip.
6. Check the tightness of all other hoses and connections.
7. Fill the system with coolant (see page 7 for anti-freeze solution) through the filler orifice until completely full.
8. Refit the filler cap.

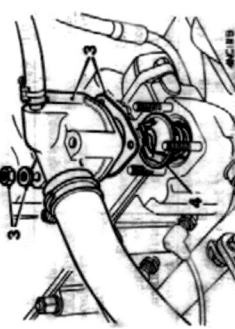

DRIVE BELT

Remove and refit 26.20.07

Removing

1. Slacken the alternator adjusting link nut and screw.
2. Slacken the alternator pivot bolts and nuts.
3. Push the alternator towards the engine to slacken the drive belt.
4. Withdraw the drive belt from the engine.

Refitting

5. Reverse the procedure in 1 to 4.
6. Tension the drive belt as described in 'MAINTENANCE'.

FAN BLADES AND PULLEY

Remove and refit 26.25.01

Removing

1. Slacken the alternator pivot bolts and nuts.
2. Slacken the alternator adjusting link screw and nut.
3. Push the alternator towards the engine to slacken the drive belt.
4. Withdraw the drive belt from the engine.
5. Unscrew the four set screws to release the fan and pulley from the water pump.

Refitting

6. Reverse the procedure in 1 to 5.
7. Tension the drive belt as described in 'MAINTENANCE'.

THERMOSTAT

Remove and refit 26.45.01

Removing

WARNING: If the cooling system is hot, remove the filler cap slowly to release the pressure gradually from the cooling system.
1. Remove the filler cap.
2. Slacken the clip and disconnect the bottom hose from the radiator and part drain the cooling system.
3. Remove the three nuts to release the housing and its joint washer from the cylinder head.
4. Withdraw the thermostat from the cylinder head.

Refitting

5. Reverse the procedure in 2 to 4, noting that the nominal temperature in degrees Celsius (Centigrade) at which the thermostat opens is stamped on the base of the thermostat bulb.
6. Refill the cooling system.

THERMOSTAT

Test 26.45.09

1. If the thermostat is stuck in the open position it is faulty and must be renewed.
2. Place the thermostat in a container of water, noting the water temperature at which the thermostat opens. The nominal temperature in degrees Celsius (centigrade) at which the thermostat opens is stamped on the base of the thermostat bulb.

WATER PUMP

Remove and refit 26.50.01

Removing

1. Drain the cooling system.
2. Disconnect the battery.
3. Disconnect the wire from the thermal transmitter (if fitted).
4. Slacken the alternator adjusting link screw.
5. Slacken the alternator adjusting link nut.
6. Slacken the alternator pivot bolts and nuts.
7. Push the alternator towards the engine and remove the drive belt.
8. Remove the pivot bolts and adjusting link and move the alternator aside.
9. Slacken the clips and release the bottom radiator hose from the water pump and heater connecting pipe.
10. Unscrew the four set screws to release the water pump and its joint washer from the cylinder block and detach the pump.
11. Unscrew the four set screws to release the fan and pulley from the water pump hub.

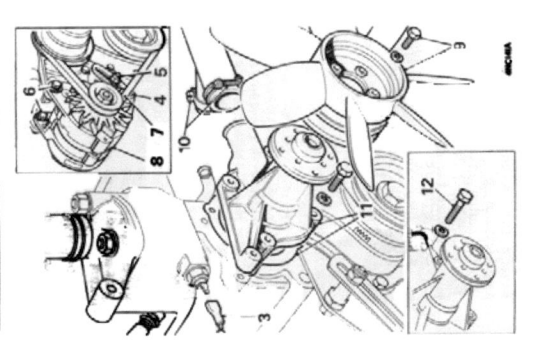

12 Remove the bolt adjacent to the water pump from the pump.

Refitting
13 Reverse the procedure in 2 to 12.
14 Tension the drive as described in 'MAINTENANCE'.
15 Refill the cooling system.

CLUTCH ASSEMBLY   33.10.01

Remove and refit

Service tool: 18G 1195

Removing

1. Release the clutch slave cylinder from the clutch housing.
2. Withdraw the slave cylinder from its push-rod and support it clear of the power unit.
3. Remove the starter securing bolts, withdraw the starter.
4. Support the gearbox, remove the nuts, bolts, and spring washers securing the flywheel housing and withdraw the gearbox assembly from the engine.
5. Mark the clutch and flywheel for reassembly.
6. Remove the clutch securing screws and lift the clutch assembly off its two locating dowels.

Refitting

7. Reverse the procedure in 1 to 6 as necessary, noting:
   a. The clutch driven plate is marked 'FLYWHEEL SIDE'.
   b. Centralize the driven plate, using tool 18G 1195.
   c. When fitting the flywheel housing bolts, fit the bolts at the top R.H. and bottom L.H. first.

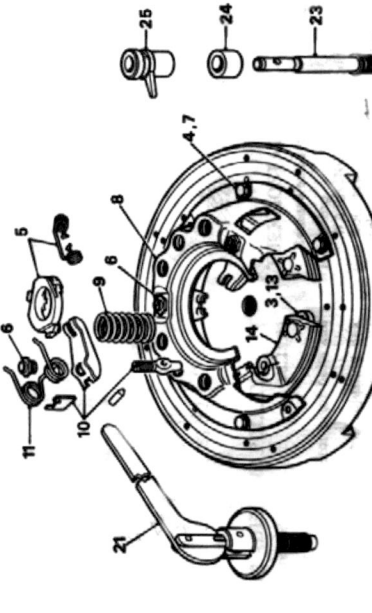

CLUTCH ASSEMBLY   33.10.08

Overhaul

Service tool: 18G 99A

1. Remove the clutch, see 33.10.01.
2. Mark the pressure plate lugs, the release levers and the release lever plate in relation to the clutch cover for correct reassembly.
3. 9 in clutch: Select three code 3 spacers from tool 18G 99 A on the tool base. 8 in clutch: select three code 2 spacers from tool 18G 99 A and place them in positions 'C' on the tool base.
4. Place the clutch assembly on top of the spacers and bolt it to the tool base.
5. Disconnect the retaining springs from the release lever plate, lift off the plate and remove the retaining springs.
6. Unscrew the three adjusting nuts from the eyebolts.
   NOTE: These nuts are staked for security.
7. Unscrew, progressively and in diagonal sequence, the bolts securing the clutch assembly to the tool.
8. Lift off the clutch cover.
9. Lift off the thrust springs.
10. Remove each release lever by raising the lever, tilting the strut and lifting the eyebolt.
11. Remove the release lever springs from the clutch cover.
12. Renew any components which are worn or damaged.
13. 9 in clutch: Position three code 3 spacers in positions 'D' on tool 18G 99 A.
    8 in clutch: Position three code 2 spacers in positions 'C' on tool 18G 99 A.
14. Place the clutch pressure plate on top of the spacers.
15. Assemble the release levers, eyebolts and struts to the pressure plate, lubricating their working surfaces with high-melting-point grease.
16. Position the thrust springs on the pressure plate.
17. Fit the release lever springs to the clutch cover.
18. Position the clutch cover on the pressure springs.
19. Bolt the clutch cover onto the tool base.
20. Fit the adjusting nuts to the eyebolts and tighten them until they are level with the tops of the eyebolts.
21. Screw the actuator into the centre of the tool base and settle the clutch mechanism by operating the actuator several times.
22. Remove the actuator.
23. Fit the centre pillar to the tool base.
24. 9 in clutch: Fit the code 7 spacer to the centre pillar with its counterbored end downwards.
    8 in clutch: Fit the code 6 spacer to the centre pillar with its counterbored end downwards.
25. Fit the gauge finger to the centre pillar.
26. Adjust the eyebolt adjusting nuts until the gauge finger just touches each release lever.
27. Remove the centre pillar assembly and re-settle the clutch mechanism, using the actuator.
28. Re-check the release lever heights, using the gauge finger, and re-set them if necessary.
29. Stake the adjusting nuts into the slots in the eyebolts.
30. Fit the retaining springs to the release levers so that the spring ends point outwards from the clutch centre.
31. Fit the release lever plate and secure it with the retaining springs.
32. Remove the clutch assembly from the tool.
33. Refit the clutch, see 33.10.01.

RELEASE BEARING 33.25.12

Remove and refit

Service tool: 18G 1195

Removing

1. Release the clutch slave cylinder from the clutch housing.
2. Withdraw the slave cylinder from its push-rod and tie it clear of the power unit.
3. Remove the starter securing bolts, withdraw the starter.
4. Support the gearbox, remove the nuts, bolts, and spring washers securing the flywheel housing and withdraw the gearbox assembly from the engine.
5. Remove the two retainers from the release bearing.
6. Remove the release bearing.

Refitting

7. Reverse the procedure in 1 to 6 as necessary, noting:
   a. Coat the rear half of the release bearing bore with Duckhams Laminoid 'O' Grease or equivalent.
   b. Ensure that the clutch driven plate is central, using tool 18G 1195.
   c. When fitting the flywheel housing bolts, fit the bolts at the top R.H. and bottom L.H. first.

SERVICE PRECAUTIONS 86.01.01

Polarity
Ensure that the correct battery polarity is maintained at all times: reversed battery or charger connections will damage the alternator rectifiers.

Battery connections
The battery must never be disconnected while the engine is running.

Testing semi-conductor devices
Never use an ohmmeter of the type incorporating a hand-driven generator for checking the rectifiers or the transistors.

Battery boosting and charging
CAUTION: The following precautions must be observed to avoid the possibility of serious damage to the charging system or electrical components of the vehicle.

Battery boosting: When connecting an additional battery to boost a discharged battery in the vehicle, ensure that:
- the booster battery is of the same nominal voltage as the vehicle battery.
- the interconnecting cables are of sufficient capacity to carry starting current.
- the cables are interconnected one at a time and to the booster battery first.
- the cables are connected between the battery terminals in the following order:

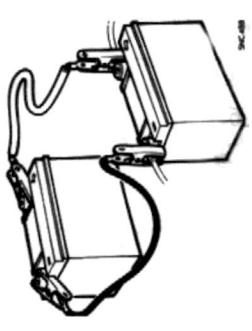

First, + (Positive) to + (Positive) and then – (Negative) to – (Negative).

- the engine speed is reduced to 1000 rev/min or below before disconnecting the boost battery. The vehicle battery must never be disconnected while the engine is running.

Battery charging: When charging the battery in the vehicle from an outside source such as a trickle charger ensure that:
- the charger voltage is the same as the nominal voltage of the battery.
- the charger positive (+) lead is connected to the positive (+) terminal of the battery.
- the charger negative (–) lead is connected to the negative (–) terminal of the battery.

TESTING THE CHARGING CIRCUIT 86.01.02

Test conditions: Alternator drive belt adjusted correctly, battery terminals clean and tight, battery in good condition (electrolyte consistent), specific gravity readings and cables and terminal connections in the charging circuit in good condition.

Test	Procedure	Remarks
1 To check that battery voltage is reaching the alternator.	Remove the cable connector from the alternator. Connect the negative side of a voltmeter to earth. Switch on the ignition. Connect the positive side of the voltmeter to each of the alternator cable connectors in turn.	a If battery voltage is not available at the 'IND' cable connector, check the no-charge warning lamp bulb and the warning lamp circuit for continuity. b If battery voltage is not available at the main charging cable connector, check the circuit between the battery and the alternator for continuity. c If battery voltage is available at the cable connectors mentioned in 'a' and 'b' proceed with Test 2.
2 Alternator test	Re-connect the cable connector to the alternator. Disconnect the brown cable with eyelet from the terminal on the starter motor solenoid. Connect an ammeter between the brown cable and the terminal on the starter motor solenoid. Connect a voltmeter across the battery terminals. Run the engine at 6,000 alternator rev/min and wait until the ammeter reading is stable.	a If a zero ammeter reading is obtained, remove and overhaul the alternator. b If an ammeter reading below 10 amperes and a voltmeter reading between 13.6 and 14.4 volts is obtained, and if battery is in a low state of charge, check the alternator performance on a test bench. c If an ammeter reading below 10 amperes and a voltmeter reading below 13.6 volts is obtained, remove the alternator and renew the voltage regulator. d If an ammeter reading above 10 amperes and a voltmeter reading above 14.4 volts is obtained renew the voltage regulator.

4. Remove the screw retaining the capacitor (when fitted) to the end bracket.
5. Remove the screw retaining the surge protection diode to the end bracket.
6. Early models: Remove the two screws retaining the brush moulding and the one screw retaining the regulator to the end bracket and remove the assembly.
   Later models: Remove the two screws retaining the brush box moulding and the regulator to the end bracket and remove the assembly.
7. Remove the screw retaining the rectifier earthing link to the slip-ring end bracket.
8. Using a thermostatically controlled soldering iron, or a standard iron and a thermal shunt attached to the diode pin, unsolder each of the three stator cables in turn from the rectifier.
9. Slacken the rectifier retaining nut and remove the assembly from the end bracket.
10. Mark the drive-end bracket, the stator lamination pack, and the slip-ring end bracket, to assist reassembly.
11. Remove the three through-bolts and withdraw the slip-ring end bracket and the stator lamination pack.
12. Remove the 'O' ring from inside the slip-ring end bracket.
13. Remove the nut and withdraw the pulley and fan from the rotor shaft.
14. Remove the pulley key and withdraw the distance piece from the rotor shaft.
15. Press the rotor out of the drive-end bracket bearing.
16. Withdraw the distance piece from the drive end of the rotor.
17. Remove the circlip to release the bearing, bearing cover-plates, 'O' ring, and felt washer from the drive-end bracket.

Inspection
18. Check the bearings for wear and roughness; if necessary, repack the bearing with Shell Alvania RA grease. To renew the slip-ring end bearing, unsolder the two field connections from the slip-ring and withdraw the

continued

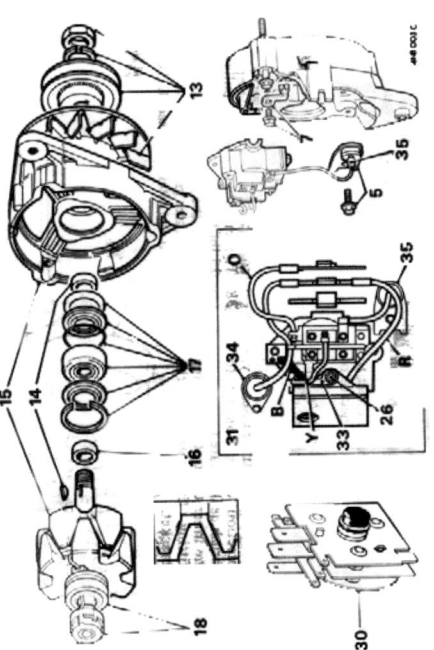

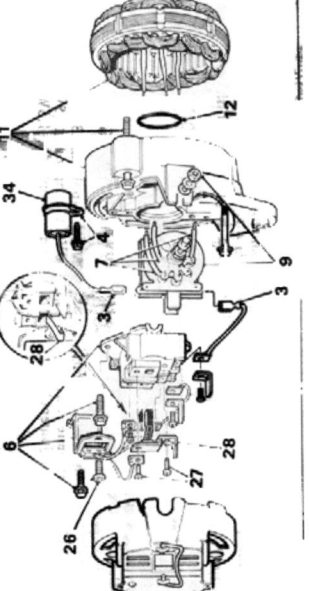

ALTERNATOR
Overhaul 86.10.08

Dismantling
1. Remove the alternator, see 86.10.02.
2. Remove the two screws to release the end cover from the alternator.
3. Note the fitted position and colour of the electrical leads connected to the rectifier spade terminals, and disconnect the leads.

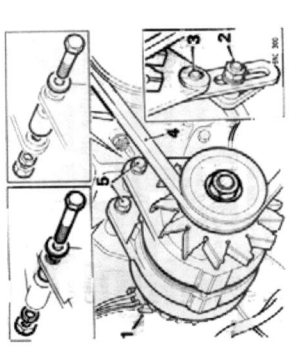

ALTERNATOR
Remove and refit 86.10.02

Removing
1. Release the spring clip and withdraw the multi-connector from the alternator end cover.
2. Slacken the adjustment link nut.
3. Remove the bolt retaining the adjustment link to the alternator.
4. Slacken the alternator pivot bolts and remove the drive belt.
5. Support the alternator and remove the alternator pivot bolts. Note the position of the spacer on the front pivot bolt.
6. Remove the alternator from the engine.
7. Hold the alternator pulley in a soft jawed vice and remove the pulley retaining nut.
8. Withdraw the pulley and fan from the alternator.

Refitting
9. Fit the fan and pulley to the alternator and tighten the retaining nut to 25 lbf ft (3.46 kgf m, 33 Nm).
10. Reverse the procedure in 1 to 6, adjusting the drive belt tension (see 'MAINTENANCE').

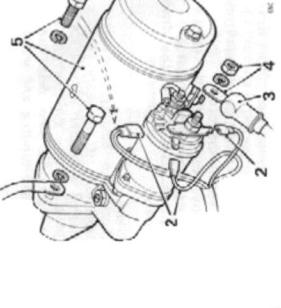

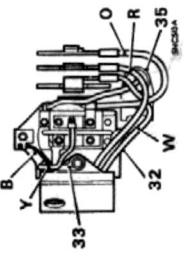

slip-ring and the bearing from the rotor shaft. Reassemble, ensuring that the shielded side of the bearing faces the slip-ring assembly. Use Fry's H.T.3 solder to remake the field connections to the slip-ring.

19 Clean the surfaces of the slip-ring, removing any evidence of burning using very fine glass paper.

20 Check the insulation of the field windings, connecting the test equipment (see DATA) between one of the slip-rings and one of the rotor lobes.

21 Check the field windings against the specifications given in DATA, connecting the test equipment (see DATA) between the slip-rings.

22 Check the stator windings for continuity, connecting the test equipment (see DATA) between any two of the stator cables, then repeating the test using the third cable in place of one of the first two.

23 Check the stator winding insulation, connecting the test equipment (see DATA) between any one of the three stator cables and the stator lamination pack.

24 Check the nine diodes, connecting the test equipment (see DATA) between each diode pin and its associated heatsink in turn, then reverse the test equipment connections. Current should flow in one direction only. Renew the rectifier assembly if a diode is faulty, see 30.

25 Check the brush spring pressure (see DATA) when the brush face is pushed in flush with the brushbox face.

26 Remove the screw retaining the regulator to the brushbox.

27 Note the fitted position and colour of the electrical leads and remove the screws and terminal strips retaining the brushes.

28 Remove the brushes, note the leaf spring fitted at the side of the inner brush.

29 Check the brushes for length. Renew the brushes and/or springs if not as quoted in DATA.

Reassembling
30 If renewing the rectifier ensure that the correct replacement is fitted, see illustration. Note that similar type rectifiers are not interchangeable.

Regulator electrical connections
31 BLACK lead earth (when fitted): connect to the brush box.
YELLOW lead positive terminal: connect on outside of the outer brush retaining plate.
RED lead battery positive: connect to the middle positive spade connector of the rectifier assembly.
32 WHITE lead (when fitted) to the rectifier second spade connection.
33 Connecting strip to the regulator.
34 Capacitor (when fitted): connect to the middle spade of rectifier assembly.
35 Surge protection diode: connect to the outer brush as illustrated.
36 Support the inner track of the bearing when refitting the rotor to the drive-end bracket.

37 Use 'M' grade 45-55 tin-lead solder to remake the stator to rectifier connections.
38 Tighten the alternator pulley nut to 25 lbf ft (3.46 kgf m, 34 Nm).
39 Check the alternator output against the figures given in DATA.
40 Refit the alternator, see 86.10.02.

STARTER MOTOR
Type M45G

Remove and refit   86.60.01

Removing
1 Disconnect the battery.
2 Disconnect the three cables from the terminal blades on the solenoid.
3 Pull back the rubber cover from the terminal on the solenoid.
4 Remove the terminal retaining nut and washer and detach the cable.
5 Remove the two bolts to release the starter motor from the engine.

Refitting
6 Reverse the procedure in 1 to 5.

DATA
Alternator output at 14V:
 16 ACR ....   34A at 6,000 alternator rev/min
 18 ACR ....   43A at 6,000 alternator rev/min
Minimum brush length .. 0.2 in (5 mm) protruding beyond brush box moulding
Brush spring pressure .   3 to 4 N, 9 to 13 ozf, 255 to 369 gf when brush is pushed in flush with brush box face.

Field winding:
Resistance at 20°C (68°F):
 16 ACR ....   3.3 ohms ± 5%
 18 ACR ....   3.2 ohms ± 5%
Current flow at 12V 3A
Insulation test equipment .. 110V a.c. supply and 15W test lamp
Stator windings:
Continuity test equipment .. 12V d.c. supply and 36W test lamp
Insulation test equipment .. 110V a.c. supply and 15W test lamp
Diode current test equipment .. 12V d.c. supply and 1.5W test lamp

STARTER MOTOR SOLENOID

Remove and refit 86.60.08

Removing
1. Disconnect the battery.
2. Disconnect the three cables from the terminal blades on the solenoid.
3. Pull back the rubber cover from the terminal on the solenoid.
4. Remove the terminal retaining nut and washer and detach the cable.
5. Remove the nut and washer securing the connecting link to the terminal 'STA' on the solenoid.
6. Remove the two screws and washers securing the solenoid to the starter.
7. Remove the solenoid coil unit from the starter motor drive end bracket.
8. Withdraw the spring from the plunger.
9. Lift the operating plunger from the engagement lever and withdraw it from the drive end bracket.
10. Remove the nut and washer retaining the terminal blade to the solenoid and remove the blade.

Refitting
11. Lubricate the operating surfaces of the plunger connecting link and engagement lever with Shell SB2628 grease (temperate and cold climates) or Shell Retinax A grease (hot climates).
12. Reverse the procedure in 1 to 10.

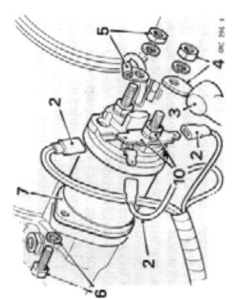

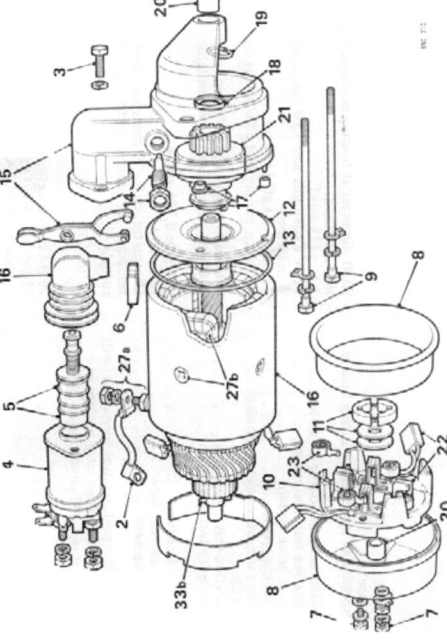

STARTER MOTOR —
Lucas Type M45G (Pre-engaged)

Overhaul 86.60.13

Dismantling
1. Remove the starter motor, see 86.60.01.
2. Disconnect the link between the solenoid 'STA' terminal and the yoke terminal.
3. Remove the two set screws and washers securing the solenoid to the drive end bracket.
4. Withdraw the solenoid coil unit from the drive end bracket.
5. Lift the solenoid plunger and return spring from the engagement lever.
6. Remove the rubber sealing block from the drive end bracket.
7. Remove the retaining nut and set screw securing the cover to the commutator end bracket.
8. Withdraw the cover and sealing ring.
9. Unlock and remove the two through-bolts.
10. Separate the commutator end bracket from the yoke, disengaging the field coil brushes from their brush boxes to release the commutator end bracket from the yoke.
11. Remove the brake-shoes, springs, steel and fibre thrust washers from the commutator end bracket.
12. Withdraw the yoke and field coil assembly from the armature and intermediate bracket.
13. Remove the sealing ring from the intermediate bracket.
14. Slacken the locknut and remove the engagement lever pivot pin from the drive end bracket.
15. Separate the drive end bracket and engagement lever from the armature, intermediate bracket and drive assembly.
16. Remove the bellows-type seal from the engagement lever.
17. Remove the seals from the drive end bracket.
18. Drive the thrust collar rearwards off the jump ring.
19. Remove the jump ring and withdraw the thrust collar, roller clutch drive and intermediate bracket from the armature shaft.

Inspection
20. Check for excessive side-play of the armature shaft in the bushes, renewing the bushes if necessary, noting:
   a. Prior to fitting, new self-lubricating porous-bronze bushes must be soaked for 20 minutes in 'Shell Turbo 41' or new engine oil.
   b. Press the new bushes into position, using a shouldered, polished mandrel of the dimension given in DATA.
21. Check that the roller clutch takes up drive instantaneously in one direction and revolves freely in the other direction. Ensure that the drive assembly moves freely along the armature shaft helices.
22. Check that the brushes move freely in the brush boxes. Renew brushes that are worn to the dimension given in DATA.
23. Using a new brush, check the pressure of each spring in turn against the specification given in DATA, renewing the spring if necessary.
24. Check the insulation of the brush boxes by connecting the test equipment (see DATA) between a clean part of the commutator end bracket and each of the two insulated brush boxes in turn.
25. Check the field coil insulation by connecting the test equipment (see DATA) between the yoke terminal and the yoke. Ensure that the brushes are not touching the yoke.

continued

26 Check the field coil continuity by connecting the test equipment (see DATA) between the two field brushes.
27 If the field coils are still suspect, prove them by substitution:
   a Remove the nut(s), washers and insulation pieces from the yoke mounted terminal stud, noting the order for reassembly.
   b Remove the pole-shoe retaining screws to release the pole-shoes, field coils and the inter-coil connector to yoke insulation piece, noting its position for reassembly.
   c Fit the pole-shoes to the new field coils and reassemble. Position tightening screws lightly. Position the inter-coil connector to yoke insulation piece and install the yoke terminal insulation pieces, washers and nut(s). Tighten the pole-shoe screws to 20 lbf ft (2.76 kgf m, 27.11 Nm).
28 Check the armature shaft. If the shaft is bent or distorted the armature must be renewed.
29 Clean the commutator brush surface, using very fine emery cloth and wipe the surface with a petrol-moistened cloth. If necessary, the commutator surface may be skimmed providing a finished surface can be obtained before exceeding the minimum diameter (see DATA). Do not undercut the insulation.
30 Check the armature insulation, connecting the test equipment (see DATA) between one of the commutator segments and the armature shaft.
31 Check the armature for short-circuited windings, using specialized armature testing (Growler) equipment. In the absence of this equipment a suspect armature must be checked by substitution.
32 Check the solenoid windings against the specification given in DATA, connecting the test equipment (see DATA) between the solenoid terminal 'STA' and the solenoid body. If the test is unsatisfactory, renew the solenoid unit.

Reassembling

33 Reverse the procedure in 2 to 19, noting:
   a Lubricate the armature shaft helices, the moving parts of the engagement lever, the outer surface of the roller-clutch housing with Shell SB 2628 grease (temperate and cold climates); Shell Retinax A grease (hot climates).
   b Ensure that the cross peg in the armature shaft engages in the brake-shoe slots.
   c Smear the end of the solenoid plunger in contact with the return spring with clean engine oil.
   d Before connecting the link between the solenoid and the starter, set the position of the drive pinion as follows:
      i Connect the solenoid terminal 'STA' to earth.
      ii Connect a 6-volt supply between the solenoid operating 'Lucar' terminal and earth.
      iii Press the pinion lightly back towards the armature to take up any slack in the drive operating mechanism.
      iv Rotate the engagement lever pivot pin (with the arrow pointing above the horizontal) to set the pinion to thrust collar clearance at the figure given in DATA.
      v Apply a sealing compound such as goldsize to the threads of the pivot pin before tightening the locknut.
34 Mount the starter motor on a test bench and check its performance against the specification given in DATA.
35 Refit the starter motor, see 86.60.01.

DATA

Armature:
Diameter of mandrel for fitting bushes . . . Shaft diameter at bearing position + 0.0005 in (0.012 mm)
Minimum commutator diameter . . . . . . 1.5 in (38 mm)
Insulation test equipment . . . . 110V a.c. supply and 15W test lamp
Minimum brush length . . . . ⁴⁄₁₆ in (8 mm)
Brush spring pressure . . . . 42 ozf, 1.2 kgf, 11 N
Brush box insulation test equipment . . . 110V a.c. supply and 15W test lamp
Field coils:
Insulation test equipment . . . . 110V a.c. supply and 15W test lamp
Continuity test equipment . . . . 110V a.c. supply and 15W test lamp
Solenoid:
Winding resistance . . . . 0.605 to 0.725 ohms
Winding current flow . . . . 16 to 20A
Test equipment . . . . Ohmmeter, or 0–20 range moving-coil ammeter in series with a 12V d.c. supply

Starter motor performance (obtained with a 12V 128 Ah (20-hour rate) battery in a 70 per cent charged condition at 20°C (68°F):
Lock torque . . . . 29 lbf ft (4.0 kgf m, 39.30 Nm) with 940 A
Running torque . . . . 11 lbf ft (1.5 kgf m, 14.9 Nm) at 1,000 rev/min with 540 A
Light running current . 100 A at 5,000 to 6,000 rev/min